CHORLTON-CUM-HARDY

BRITAIN IN OLD PHOTOGRAPHS

CHORLTON-CUM-HARDY

CLIFF HAYES

SUTTON PUBLISHING LIMITED

Sutton Publishing Limited
Phoenix Mill · Thrupp · Stroud
Gloucestershire · GL5 2BU

First published 1999

Title page: Shops opposite the Lloyd Hotel, 1930s.

British Library Cataloguing in Publication Data
A catalogue record for this book is available from the
British Library.

ISBN 0-7509-2065-3

Typeset in 10/11 Bembo.
Typesetting and origination by
Sutton Publishing Limited.
Printed in Great Britain by
Ebenezer Baylis, Worcester.

The Horse & Jockey Inn, *c.* 1920. The right-hand side of the black and white building was a private
residence with its own garden and fence.

CONTENTS

ACKNOWLEDGEMENTS

Thanks to Philip Lloyd for the use of his wonderful collection of postcards of old Chorlton, and his time and patience to talk to me about them, answering all my queries. Without men like Mr Lloyd much local history would be lost forever. A big thank you to Steve Henderson, who is also a collector of postcards from Chorlton's past and who has a great interest in and knowledge of its history. He has lent me many of his postcards and rare items from his collection, and his photographs from the '70s and '80s, which I have used, make the book a more complete record of the area. Steve is also a printer 'like what I used to be' – a Gentleman of the Industry of Knowledge, as my night-school teacher would say of the compositors of the printing industry. Thanks also to Bill Newton, librarian, now resident at Old Trafford Library, for his help and advice, to Gordon Coltas of 'Locofotos' for permission to use his railway pictures and to Chris Makepeace for the use of photographs on p. 39. Mention must be made of a good friend, Jed McCann of Ashton, who has helped to get some of the older and more faded photographs quite a bit clearer. Thanks too to Mike Shah of Chorlton Service Station for his help.

A special thanks to Vicky, her mum and dad, and all the staff at Chorlton Bookshop who believe so positively in the value and power of the written word and who really commissioned this book. My long-time friend Brian Barlow, from Beech Road Second-Hand Bookshop, has helped me put together a collection of local history books. Thanks to Tom Waghorn and the *Manchester Evening News* for the photographs of the Bee Gees and Sir Robert Mark. Thanks also to Pearson Television and Thames, for permission to include the 'Chorlton and the Wheelies' photograph.

A special thanks must be recorded to my wife, Sylvia, who took a lot of the harder work out of the book by helping more than ever with the paperwork and for typing and editing my scribbling and jottings into the book you see before you.

INTRODUCING CHORLTON-CUM-HARDY

'Ton' in Middle English meant 'dwellings surrounded by a ditch or fence'. The 'Chorl' part of the name could came from 'ceorls', meaning peasant or poor people. 'Churls' were farm workers who worked for their keep and board, and later were people above a serf but not as elevated as thanes or freemen. So Chorlton can mean 'The fortified dwellings of the Churls, who work for no money'. Given the agricultural nature of the area and the time the name was first recorded, 'farm workers who are kept, housed and not paid in money' seems the most likely. 'Cum' is the old word for nearby, and Hardy was the name of the area to the back of Chorlton Green, where Hardy Lane is now, and meant 'by the woods'. The whole area was once covered by a wood known as Arden Wood and Hardy could have come from that. The 'cum-Hardy' was added to avoid confusion with Chorlton-on-Medlock, which used to be called Chorlton Row.

Chorlton is first mentioned in around AD 700, making it one of the oldest names in the area, and as there was no major crossing of the River Mersey here it was considered a backwater and useful only for growing produce. The area was part of the domain of Withington until the Norman Conquest, when the Barlows and Traffords took up ownership. Later the Mosley family, Lords of Manchester, made their residence at Hough End Hall, and the Chorlton area broke away to form its own township. It still remained an area of farms, large houses and cottages until the coming of the railway in 1880, when the idea of living in a country area and commuting to work became a reality. The original centre of village life was Chorlton Green, but as the railway station and later the trams did not go too near there, the centre of life moved to the Manchester Road/Wilbraham Road junction.

Chorlton-cum-Hardy was part of the Chorlton (on Medlock) Poor Law Union in 1837. The passing of the Poor Law in 1834 meant that townships were forced to band together to afford to look after the rising number of poor people and orphans. In 1876 the four townships of Chorlton, Withington, Didsbury and Burnage were formed into a Local Board District with all the authority needed to rule themselves. The three

Chorlton members, of the fifteen-member board were first elected in November 1876. This Local Board lasted only eighteen years, ending in December 1894, and was replaced by Withington Urban District Council, again with three Chorlton representatives. This UDC became part of Manchester on 15 August 1904, when Royal Assent was given to one of the Manchester Extension Bills.

The area that we consider as Chorlton-cum-Hardy today is fairly well defined, and is surrounded by the following areas:

FIRSWOOD takes its name from Firs Farm, which once stood where St Hilda's Junior School stands today, and was named after a wood of fir trees that stood near Kings Road. Nearly all the houses were built in the 1920s when land was released by the Trafford family, and were privately developed.

Firswood was defined as the area between Seymour Grove and Greatstone Road one way and Kings Road to Manchester Road the other, which is the area the farm covered. Many think of the area as being part of Chorlton, and though most people give the postal address as Stretford, it is part of Old Trafford.

HOUGH END means 'where the Lord's Manor is', and it was just that, the place where the Mosley family made their home. Before the Mosleys the area east of Nell Lane was outside Chorlton, but then it came within the Chorlton boundary – later still moving away again, back to Withington.

HULME comes from the word 'Holmr', which in Saxon times meant 'small hill or rising ground'. There were at one time five Hulmes around Manchester, the other four taking on prefixes to distinguish them from each other. Our Hulme was probably the most important and therefore kept its simple form.

Hulme township was described as the area between the River Medlock and Cornbrook with the River Irwell as its western boundary. It was one of the six original areas that made up the town of Manchester when it was officially constituted in 1838, Chorlton Row, Beswick, Ardwick and Cheetham all joining Manchester.

Hulme was important enough to have its own independent system of government until it formed part of the original town of Manchester.

MOSS SIDE is a simple and popular name. There are at least six other Moss Sides in Lancashire though none as famous or well known as this one. Moss Side means 'at the side of the moss', and there was a mossy area here. The soil is very peaty and if you dig out and compress the soil it should be possible to burn it on open grates, as the poor of the area did long ago. The area was first noted as Mossyde in 1530, and the name in its present form dates from 1594. Moss Side was a separate township and one with considerable powers; it ran its own schools, libraries and had its own council until 1885, when it was taken in on the first enlargement of Manchester's boundaries.

OLD TRAFFORD, which stretches from Upper Chorlton Road to the River Irwell (Ship Canal and Salford Docks), was originally Trafford. We know that King Cnut fought a battle over this land and gave it to his right-hand man, who became Ralph Trafford in about 1025. The name could come from the Old English 'troh', 'a hollow or trough', or 'the ford in a hollow', which would have described the place where today the Metrolink is just about to cross the Irwell and into Salford. There is some thought that Trafford is a version of Stretford – 'the ford with the Roman road' (Streta).

When the Bridgewater Canal was being built in the 1760s, the Trafford family decided to move out of the family hall, which was at Trafford Bar. They turned their hunting lodge, Wittleswick Hall, which was inside Trafford Park, into the family seat, which became Trafford Hall. The house they left behind became Trafford Old Hall and the area was referred to as Old Trafford (as opposed to new Trafford, which was the park). Old Trafford was owned and dominated by the Trafford family and was never a township in its own right but came under Stretford. When the Local Government Act of 1972 created the Greater Manchester County, Trafford was formed as an MBC, and since 1974 the area has been run from Sale.

The boundary between Stretford and Manchester was a mercurial thing, being drawn on Corn Brook, which has changed its course once or twice in history. When the area was built on there were houses with their front doors in Stretford and their back doors in Manchester. There are stories like that of the man who had to put out his dustbins through the front door as his back yard was in Manchester and he was paying Stretford rates, and the householder who moved his electricity meter into the outside toilet because electricity was cheaper in Manchester.

WHALLEY RANGE, originally called Jackson's Moss, was bought by a financier called Samuel Brooks in the early 1800s from the de Trafford family. Because he had come to live in Manchester from Whalley in Lancashire he decided to call the area Whalley Range after his home town. He also gave us Brooks's Bar and, when he set up house in Sale, Brooklands. Whalley Range is on the Manchester side of Upper Chorlton Road, the boundary running down the centre of that road – but has never ruled itself, always being part of the Moss Side area.

The areas and footpaths of Old Chorlton, *c.* 1845, taken from a map drawn by John Lloyd.

THE MAKING OF CHORLTON-CUM-HARDY

The Arden Forest covered the whole of south Lancashire including Chorlton. The River Mersey (the word Mersey means boundary) ran right through that forest. The river at this point was prone to rising fast after rain, and a natural flood area developed, which became known as the Ees. The Chorlton Ees, and the Stretford and Sale Ees are still there today (an Ees or Eyes is an area of land that floods when rivers rise), and it was this rich open land that led to the development of the place called Chorlton. As the trees were cleared more land became available to cultivate and workers were needed to work that land, so we find those workers building their dwelling together for safety and we find the start of Chorlton. Most local historians put the start of the village in about AD 620, and while I cannot find any hard evidence to point to that date, neither can I find anything to really suggest any other. Certainly by the 800s there is evidence that a community was living and working in the Chorlton Green area. As I have said there was never a major crossing of the River Mersey at this point. The river was too unpredictable at Barlow and Chorlton, and there were already recognised crossings at Stretford and at Cheadle so there was no need for another crossing. It is said that highwaymen, including the famous Dick Turpin and our own local 'Gentleman of the Road' Edward Higgins, knew how to cross the Mersey safely at Chorlton and thus shake off any pursuers, but these were the exception.

Our Chorlton of today is made up of four major areas, once well defined but now merged. MARTLEDGE was the area to the north that ran from Sandy Lane up to the Old Trafford border at Upper Chorlton Road. Martledge was east of Manchester Road and included the area known as Manley Park, Dark Farm and Hobson's Hall, another farm in the area. The area where the Seymour Hotel stands, and where Manchester Road ends and Seymour Grove begins, was known as West Point. The FLASHES, with its ponds and streams, was the area at the north end of Oswald Road above Kensington Road. This area was nothing but open fields and streams, with Black Brook marking its northern extreme and Edge Lane marking the southern. Longford Brook ran through the area, and 'The Isles' was a name given to the place where the brook had created a number of ponds on the clay soil. CHORLTON itself was the area south of Edge Lane and west of Barlow Moor Road, north of Hardy Lane, but including what is now the nature reserve and Chorltonville.

HARDY was the area south of Hardy Lane and included Barlow Moor and Barlow Moor Hall, the seat of the very ancient family the Barlows. The name 'Barlow' means 'the place where the boar roam', and Barlow Moor was once a bleak and windswept area of scrubland. This moor extended across Princess Parkway, and the boundary was more or less the River Mersey in West Didsbury.

Many of the old names have gone and the A-Zs of today have moved names from their original settings. The names of some of Chorlton's roads are all we have to give pointers and hints of the past.

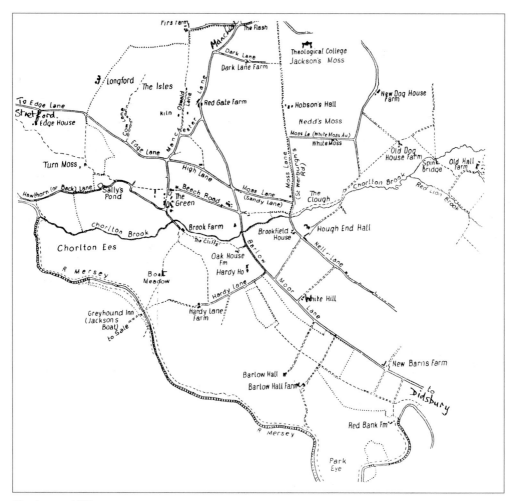

Chorlton, c. 1850.
Key: Chorlton boundary ••••; footpaths – – – –; cart tracks = = = =.

CHAPTER ONE

CHORLTON GREEN

Chorlton Green is a delightful oasis, a remnant of the common land which was once the heart of the community. The fact that it has survived is probably because the commercial centre of Chorlton moved away, removing the pressure of redevelopment. Stretford had a green but it has gone, Old Trafford had a 'green' and it too has gone, but Chorlton's has survived, although smaller than the original common land.

The Green, with a public telephone box blocking the view of the Horse & Jockey and the house next door, c. 1936. The telephone box replaced a drinking fountain. You can still the posts that surrounded the green, but they were soon to go in the 'scrap metal for war' effort only a few years away.

Chorlton Green, probably 1920s. The trees are fairly mature and the Horse & Jockey has acquired its famous black and white look. The building dates from about 1510, and although much altered and added to there are still parts remaining from the sixteenth century. The house attached to the pub was the home of the Wilton family, and it was Samuel Wilton who 'hedged in' The Green in about 1810. By the 1880s The Green was known as 'Miss Wilton's Garden', and had a high hedge round it.

The Horse & Jockey Inn, with the first signs of parking problems outside, just after the Second World War. The black and white Tudor look was not added until 1905 and the inn was extended to take in the house next door some time between the wars. This view is from a private Christmas card from the Lloyd family.

Laburnum Cottage, Chorlton Green, *c.* 1907. The cottage had formerly been Ivy Green Farm, and was pulled down in the 1960s to make way for town houses.

The lych gate of the old parish church of St Clement's, 1921. Laburnum Cottage, shown above, can be seen on the left-hand side. The church notice board can be made out quite clearly. The lych gate, which is still standing today, was paid for by William Cunliffe Brooks, the banker, in 1888, as a Jubilee gift to mark fifty years of Queen Victoria's reign. Mr Brooks was one of those who in 1860 opposed the building of a new church on Edge Lane, and whose opposition made sure that this church remained the parish church for Chorlton. This could have been because he had two one-day-old children (born 1851 and 1852) buried in the graveyard, and their tombstone, which is very well preserved, can still be seen there today. The old church has gone but the gravestones remain, some dating back to 1725.

The Green, 1904, when the Horse & Jockey had yet to have its black and white façade applied. Local children always found The Green a good place to play, and would happily pose for postcard photographers who regularly toured around taking pictures. Here they are standing next to the drinking fountain.

The top of The Green, *c.* 1905. The trees are very young, the extension to the pub is still there, and part of the building is still a private house – not the landlord's. Some say the name Horse & Jockey comes from horse racing on the Ees, but we have no written record of any races taking place there; however, there are records of horse racing on Barlow Moor which was not that far away. The inn was licensed just after 1800 to cater for those who liked to walk and enjoy the area. There were pubs nearby on Beech Road much earlier than this.

Chorlton Green, *c.* 1912. The drinking fountain can be clearly seen, and now there are benches too. After the death of Miss Wilton, the land reverted to Lord Egerton who formally gave it back to the people on 1 June 1895 as part of the celebrations on the formation of the Withington UDC. The gas light that had stood by the lych gate was moved on to The Green, by the Horse and Jockey, so instead of lighting the way for church-goers it lit the way for the drinker. There were three other gas lights around The Green (the first street lights in Chorlton), so the area was still quite well lit. Town gas arrived here in 1862 via Stretford; a main was laid along Edge Lane.

Chorlton Recreation Ground, Beech Road, 1918. The original recreation grounds were south of Beech Road. These new grounds were opened on the present site on 16 May 1896 by Lord Egerton who had given the land, after selling off the old recreation ground south of Beech Road for housing.

The Bowling Green Hotel, *c*. 1900. This building was pulled down in 1907 and the present public house was built in 1908. They say that bowls has been played on this site from as early as the 1400s and there are early references to the game on Chorlton common land in both the Barlow and Mosley family papers. Where there are people and sport there will be somewhere to provide refreshments, and we find reference to a farmhouse providing ale long before 1693 when it was granted a licence, making the Bowling Green Inn the oldest licensed premises in Chorlton. The building pictured dates from 1780, and was built to catch the trade from the people bowling and taking part in other summer activities in the area. Down the lane and past the dairy there was once a field with the wonderful name of Pig Riding Meadow.

Beech Road from the Recreation Ground, looking back to Chorlton Green, 1903. This postcard was sent by Mrs Phillips of 15 Whalley Avenue, Sandy Lane, to her friend Miss Vickers in Weaste. The Recreation Ground was behind the hedge.

The shops in Beech Road, *c.* 1914, from a 1915 postcard to Private Lloyd in bed 22 in hospital at Dore, near Sheffield. Most of the buildings seen on the card are still there today, the chemist being the one on the far right. The second-hand bookshop today is just past the lamp post and the shop on the left is now a very pleasant café. When the shops on the left were built this part of Beech Road was known as Market Place, an early attempt at a village centre. Just after the buildings were completed the railway and Wilbraham Road arrived, and the centre of Chorlton drifted away.

Beech Road, early 1920s. The post box can be made out on the pavement, marking the position of Beech Road sub-post office, opened in 1900. The charm of Beech Road and the original shop fronts mean that this area is often used for television work. Beech Road is one of the oldest roads in the area, being as old as Edge Lane and Barlow Moor Road.

Beech Road at the Barlow Moor Road end, 1910. The houses on the left were built twenty years earlier on what was the original recreation ground, and the building on the right was Beech Lodge, the gatehouse to Beech House. The beech tree that gave its name to the house and road can be seen overhanging the road in the middle of this view.

CHAPTER TWO

THE NEW CENTRE

It is interesting to speculate just how the area would have developed if Wilbraham Road had not been created in the middle of the nineteenth century. If the Mosleys had not died out, or the Blands been such spendthrifts, the Egertons would not have got hold of the land they did. The fact that the horse trams and later the railway didn't go near the old centre sealed its fate, and new Chorlton-cum-Hardy was born.

The Lloyd Hotel and the Conservative Club, c. 1900. The hotel, now known as Edward's, was built in 1870 after a deal between Mr George Lloyd, who owned the land, and Mr James Platt, who did the building. Whatever the business arrangement was (and you can see both names in brick on the Manchester Road side of the building), when Mr Platt died the name was soon changed to The Lloyd. The small hut on the left was a cabman's shelter, and it was here that horse-drawn cabs would wait for hire. In 1888 the Local Board provided a cart with hand-pump and ladder, at the request of the better-off citizens, in case there was a fire in Chorlton. It was kept next to the Lloyd Hotel so that it was near the new larger houses and businesses. I wonder if that is it in this picture, Chorlton's first fire engine.

The Public Hall, Chorlton-cum-Hardy, April 1903. Today we know it as the Conservative Club. Was it built as a Public Hall and later used by the Conservative Association, or was it the Conservatives who allowed it to be used so much that the people of Chorlton considered it their hall and 'public'? Research shows that it was built by the Conservatives, and that the hall was very popular for amateur dramatics in the late nineteenth and early twentieth centuries.

The Conservative Club, 1905. Though faded, this is a very interesting view that shows how wide and important this junction was. The gas light and clock are prominent.

To Wish you
A Happy New Year.

Christmas 1905, and this overprinted postcard was posted on 30 December with new year's greetings for 1906. Again we have the building referred to as 'The Public Hall', and the view shows the gas lamp and Methodist Church behind the Club.

On 14 March 1887 the Conservative Association of Chorlton met at The Lloyd Hotel and decided to ask Lord Egerton of Tatton for some land on which to build a club. They canvassed and raised shares in the Chorlton Conservative Club and finally in 1890 they bought the land from Lord Egerton; the foundation stone was laid on 25 April 1891. The Hall opened late in 1892 and was a rallying point for all 'new Chorltonians'.

The basement of the club seems to have had many uses and has seen more change than the rest of the building. It has been a skittle alley (October 1897), a rifle range (1904) and a bike park (1900), complete with ramp, for the parking of members' bicycles. The basement is partially used as gents' toilets and cloakrooms at the moment, and there are also beer cellars down there. An electric beer raising engine was installed, at a cost of £80, in 1920 but replaced by pumps in 1926. The club was extended in 1925, and is still the centre for many activities in the Chorlton area.

The shops on Wilbraham Road opposite The Lloyd (Edward's) Hotel, before 1900. The cabmen's hut, complete with horse-drawn hackney carriage, is on the right.

When I first moved to this area twenty-two years ago, there was an old lady living across the road who often wanted odd jobs doing. As I changed the light bulb or whatever she would tell me of her childhood and shopping in Chorlton. Her mother would take her to be fitted for boots or clothes, they would look at laces and linen and then take tea in a café, either the one on Barlow Moor Road or one in this row of shops. Come 4 o'clock and they would cross to the horse-drawn cab rank outside The Lloyd and there, as if by magic, they were joined by all their purchases for the journey home to the large house on Edge Lane. I wish I'd taken more notice of Mrs Bewley, but much of what she told me sunk in, and I appreciate it now.

As the authority of the Mosleys dwindled the estate was bought in 1751 by George Lloyd and by Samuel Egerton of Tatton. George bought land in Hulme and Chorlton, while Samuel bought Hough End, the rest of Chorlton (except the Barlow land at Hardy) and the land at Withington. Very little is known about George Lloyd, other than that he signed himself 'of Manchester', that he came from a family in Yorkshire and that he was some relative of the Mosley family, though not near enough to inherit. The Mosley family, once so powerful and intimate with the area, had by 1700 distanced themselves from Hough End, and mortgaged most of the land. Samuel Egerton bought more of the lands around Edge Lane and Longford from the executors in 1785, and when the growth of new Chorlton started it was the Egerton family who were the main landowners.

Wilbraham Road, *c.* 1904. Can you make out the gate across the road at the Edge Lane end of the road? It was there to admit only genuine residents and invited tradesmen, from the time the road was built in about 1860 until the turn of the century – although it was left open quite a lot towards the end of its life.

Wilbraham Road, 1920s. The photographer is standing outside the Conservative Club and looking towards Manchester Road. There were probably four of these ornate gas lamps in Chorlton, all at major junctions, and it sometimes makes it difficult to place old photographs. No mistake about this one, though, as that is The Lloyd Hotel on the right.

Wilbraham Road, Chorlton-cum-Hardy, c. 1905. The lady pushing the bassinet (pram) and the gentleman in the straw boater help date this view, and the young trees on the newly laid pavements help. The photographer is standing at the junction of Manchester Road and Wilbraham Road and doesn't seem to have had much trouble with the traffic, though you would if you stood there today.

Wilbraham Road, 1928 – almost the same view as the one above, but the photographer has now moved on to the pavement. Maybe he was expecting cars rushing to the garage that can be seen on the right. You can still make out where the small forecourt area used to be, and today the building is used by a potter. Where the Oxfam shop and the fish and poultry shop are today, opposite, was still private houses on this photograph.

The junction of Barlow Moor Road and Wilbraham Road from where Woolies is today, at the turn of the century. The building that houses the NatWest bank today is still to be built. These three-storeyed shops were the first commercial developments on Wilbraham Road and were given low numbers; later, when the road developed further, they had to be re-numbered twice.

The junction that was to form the very centre of the new Chorlton, this time a lot closer to the crossroads, c. 1920. You can make out the wine merchant's that was on the left-hand corner and the almost makeshift shops that lead to where Safeways is today. The tram would have turned left at this crossroads before travelling down towards High Lane and the terminal there.

The north side of the junction of Barlow Moor Road with Wilbraham Road, 1903. The trees which feature so much in later postcards have not yet been planted, and where the Bank of Scotland is today is still a private house. There are no shops or houses between the shops and the railway station, which was in the distance.

Wilbraham Road was planned by Wilbraham Egerton and he planned to call it Prince's Road. He died in 1856 and his son, William Tatton Egerton, MP for Cheshire, got down to the actual work of cutting the new way. William's son, also called Wilbraham, was born in 1832, so when the road name was changed it wasn't known if it referred to his father or son. The son became the most famous, taking over the running of the Manchester Ship Canal from Daniel Adamson in 1887 and being created Earl Egerton and Viscount Salford in Queen Victoria's Diamond Jubilee Honours in 1897.

The family name of the Earl of Latham is Wilbraham, and the use of the family surname as a Christian name would have come about because one of the daughters had married into the Egerton family. It was quite common among the aristocracy to take the mother's maiden name as one of the children's forenames, if only to stop the name dying out.

Wilbraham Road, the crossroads from the other side. The shops on the left are Quarmbies, the stationers, and an off licence today. The postcard was posted on 24 July 1904 by Meg to her friend Miss Hudson, on holiday in Colwyn Bay – telling her that life in the office wasn't so bad as Mr L. had been missing every afternoon. The card was produced for H. Burt, a local stationer in Chorlton. Their shop and newsagent's business were taken over later by Quarmbies.

Chorlton centre, from a postcard produced for Brown's Stationers, Beech Road, by that very versatile company Valentine's, late 1920s. The NatWest building is there, as is the off-licence on the corner. They say that where there is money someone will open a bank, and this junction had not one but four banks, one for each corner.

Wilbraham Road, Chorlton, looking towards Fallowfield, with Egerton Road North of the immediate left. This is the only postcard I have seen of this part of Chorlton. It is taken from the railway bridge. The first shop on the left was for many years a hardware store and is now a café bar, and the shop at the end of the parade has for many years been a florist and nursery. How many of us remember getting toys from Busy Bee toyshop!

Wilbraham Road, 1946. The part of Barlow Moor Road that is above Wilbraham Road only came into prominence when the latter was cut. Before that the main road was Manchester Road, which ran from where the library is today down to opposite St Clement's Church. The building of The Lloyd Hotel caused the first deviation; Nicholas Road and the shops opposite Edward's broke up the road; and the building of the library sealed its fate.

Wilbraham Road, late 1950s or early '60s. The photographer stood outside the post office to capture this scene. The zebra crossing with its Belisha beacons (named after Leslie Hore-Belisha, Minister for Transport) has been installed, and there is plenty of activity as deliveries are made to the shops.

Postcards from the Swinging Sixties are quite hard to find these days. The habit of sending postcards (except on holiday) had died out among the younger generation, and fewer cards were produced outside the holiday areas. Here we have two of those rare 1960s cards. *Above*: Wilbraham Road from the junction with Manchester Road, on a card posted in August 1964. Manners the Tailors, where many young gentlemen were fitted out in school uniform, is on the left, and the petrol pumps are still there on the right. *Below*: Wilbraham Road at its junction with Barlow Moor Road, 1963. William Deacon's Bank is on the extreme right.

The post office, 1907. This building stood on Wilbraham Road and was next to the present post office. Chorlton got its first office for receiving mail on 1 January 1857 and this 'post and telegraph office' opened on 20 January 1901. It was a casualty of the bombing in the Blitz of December 1940, and it was 'make-do-and-mend' opposite the library until the present post office opened on 11 December 1961.

Barlow Moor Road, c. 1908. The photographer is looking at the Wilbraham Road junction from the south. Can you make out the strange building that stands next to what is now Max Spielman's photographic shop?

Barlow Moor Road, just north of the crossroads, soon after 1900. The old Royal Oak is on the left, complete with window boxes and its porched entrance, and the Co-op shop is next door (can you remember your divi number?). Wasn't there a lot of horse muck on the roads in those days. We can see plenty of it in this picture; maybe the gardeners of Chorlton weren't so quick to run out and collect it to put on the roses.

Barlow Moor Road, from another postcard produced for Brown's of Beech Road, 1920s. The Royal Oak has been rebuilt and is the pub we know today. The bank building is new, and replaced the old one with its grand entrance. H. Frank Dawson, estate agents, occupy the upper floors of the building on the corner, and the street lights are electric.

Barlow Moor Road, 1960s. The launderette has arrived, on the right, with a dyer and cleaner next door. Audrey's is just a bit further up the road, and though the tram lines have gone, some of the overhead wire support posts remain with their electric lights attached.

Barlow Moor Road, *c.* 1919. The buildings seen here were ornate. The café on the left was a popular place to meet, or to have a welcome break while out shopping.

An open-topped tram passes the Royal Oak public house on Barlow Moor Road, *c*. 1905. Can you make out the distinctive curved roof of the Billiard Hall behind the tram? The building on the right is the original bank that stood on this corner, and the porch of the old Royal Oak can be made out just above the small boy on the pavement, near the Cycle Repair sign. This cycle repairer was strategically situated: customers could leave their bike, enjoy a quiet pint and then pick up the cycle with its puncture mended.

Barlow Moor Road at its junction with Sandy Lane, 1920. This is another card commissioned by Brown's of Beech Road. The trams received route numbers by the end of the First World War and here the No. 46 Piccadilly to Chorlton Offices via Brooks Bar is almost at the end of its journey. The first tram on this route ran in 1910, and though the trams were stopped in 1938 the lines were not lifted, probably because of the threat of war. Sure enough, when war broke out and petrol for the buses became scarce, this route was one of the first to be put back on, becoming the 46X. Just behind the hedge on the right was once the tram office, before 1915. The Macfadyen Memorial Church, with its spire and belfry, shows up well behind the trees. Electric street lighting arrived with the blessing of Manchester Corporation just after 1919.

Barlow Moor Road, looking down towards Hardy Lane from the corner of Beech Road, *c*. 1919. The line from High Lane to Southern Cemetery Gates opened as early as May 1911, but most of the traffic would have been the open-topped trams and it was a Sunday only service when it started. The houses on the right are still there today, although most are used as shops. The area to the left of the picture is where McDonalds, the garage and the Feathers Hotel are today. Before McDonalds was built the Princess Club stood here. The Feathers is quite a recent pub, having been built in the 1950s. The open space of Chorlton Park can be seen behind the tram.

Chorlton Park School playground, probably 1 September 1939. The board shows arrangements for the children from this school to be evacuated to the safety of countryside or seaside – at the time it was thought for the duration of the war.

The children march with parents and police escort to Chorlton station and onward, mostly to Fleetwood, Monday 2 September 1939. What must have been going through their minds as they headed off on this big adventure, complete with gas masks, clean shirts and two changes of underwear. The petrol sign on the right for Shell petrol at 1s 3½d per gallon would soon come down, owing to wartime shortages.

Wilbraham Road at the junction with Barlow Moor Road, *c.* 1905. By 1907, when the trams had arrived, the end of Manchester Road had become a quiet backwater, and the main route lay, as it does today, from Manchester Road down Barlow Moor Road at this point. Note the old bank still standing on the left of the picture.

Manchester Road, looking down towards Chorlton centre, 1908. The shops to the right are still there today, though the swimming baths are still to be built on the vacant land on the left. The photographer is standing where the railway line ran under Manchester Road.

Looking from the junction of Manchester Road and Barlow Moor Road up Manchester Road towards West Point, probably 1931. The Savoy Cinema has only recently opened. For some strange reason the building had the name Majestic on its façade with the Savoy sign in lights on top of it. It later became the ABC, and then the Gaumont just before it closed and became the Co-op Undertakers.

Manchester Road, 1885. This is the same view as the picture above, believe it or not. It is taken from a series of cards called 'Old Chorlton', lent to Philip Lloyd by Mrs Booth of Bramhall. The wall on the left is where the Co-op and the Billiard Hall are now, and the buildings in the distance are Red Gate Farm.

The Temperance Billiard Hall on Manchester Road, 1907. The Hall had only just opened, and indeed has a sign 'Now Open – Inspection Invited' outside. The opening of this hall was looked upon as a step forward in the fight against strong drink: sarsaparilla, lemonade and tea were available to the billiard players! The area to the left is open garden, where the cinema was built twenty years later. The windows running down the sides of the building to give 'natural light' to the players cannot be clearly seen today as the hall is hemmed in by adjacent buildings.

Ellesmere Road, off Wilbraham Road, before 1911. If you look very closely you can make out a hay rick at the top of the road. This, and the building there, were part of Hobson's Hall Farm, once marked on maps as Obson's Hall. That Hall and some of the land are preserved today as the Cricket Club at the top of Ellesmere Road.

Cavendish Road, c. 1920. We know this road today as Corkland Road, the name having changed in about 1950 to avoid confusion with the Cavendish Road running behind Withington Hospital.

Edge Lane, c. 1910. The postcard was produced for A. Harold Clarke, Photographer, from 83 Clarence Road. The gateway on the right is now Belgravia Gardens. The photograph looks towards the junction with Wilbraham Road, which joins Edge Lane on the distant right.

Edge Lane, showing the corner of Manchester Road on the right and St Clement's Church and St Clement's Road to the left. The photographer is standing in High Lane, for it is at this point that the road changes its name.

Edge Lane, 1907. The very early omnibus, from Daimler Motors of Deansgate, Manchester, ran an open-topped bus service from Stretford station into Chorlton and then on to Manchester. The passengers on the top would have had to watch out for the overhanging trees down Edge Lane.

A quiet rural scene in Edge Lane, 1906. A milk cart complete with milk boy stands in the lane delivering morning milk to the large mansions which sprang up after Stretford railway station opened in 1849. Ribbon development took place from Stretford station all the way to Chorlton, as it became fashionable for the better-off to live further out from the city, but near enough to a station to be able to commute into town for business.

Longford Hall and Gardens, 1938. If you go down Edge Lane towards Stretford you come to Longford Park, and though technically outside Chorlton, the Hall and gardens were very popular with local people. The boundary between Stretford and Chorlton is the footpath that is coming in on the right-hand side of the picture. Longford Park tennis courts stand in Chorlton, as the boundary runs through the middle of the park. The Walker family, who lived for a time at Barlow Moor Hall, moved to Longford Farm and lived here for a while before selling to John Rylands, who built the Hall we see in this picture.

A close-up view of the gardens in Longford Park, c. 1930. Nannies and mothers push their bassinettes around a beautifully tended garden, and behind are greenhouses, shelters and a café.

CHAPTER THREE

WEST POINT

The name West Point is now very little used and, indeed, most people living there today would not know you were referring to this part of Upper Chorlton Road. The area was originally called 'The Flashes', and it is thought that this came from the ponds and pools that were a feature of the area and the Black Brook that ran through it. The name West Point was given to this junction at the same time that the name Whalley Range was given to the southern side of Upper Chorlton Road. It became a well-known name as the early trams from town would terminate here, from April 1903 when the electric tram arrived in the area. There was no need to carry on to Chorlton itself as the railway station was open by then, and people could get to the city centre in seven minutes on trains running four or five times an hour.

The shops at West Point c. 1910. Edward Lloyd's newsagents is the one nearest the camera, and no doubt the postcard was on sale in the shop, along with newspapers and useful presents, as the signs outside say; there was also a lending library. We are told on the back of the card that the young chap on the left of the children is one Master William Edward Lloyd, aged eight.

Looking at the row of shops from the other direction, 1947. T. Seymour Mead's shop is on the corner, and very fitting it is too – as the road going off to the left is Seymour Grove, named after the man who set up the company, and who also left the land for Seymour Park in his will.

Upper Chorlton Road, West Point, c. 1912. Watching the world go by was a popular pastime, and the sign shows the way to Trafford Bar and Brooks's Bar. Crimsworth House is visible in the distance.

The shops at the top of Upper Chorlton Road, 1958. A remarkable record of the names of some of the shop owners are displayed on their sun awnings. The building of these shops began in 1908 and they opened in 1909, on land that had once been the garden of Darley Hall.

A close-up of Upper Chorlton Road post office, 1954. I am told that there was a cigarette machine on the wall outside which gave five cigarettes for 2d, and maybe that is what is attracting the young men in this picture.

Looking from Manchester Road at Upper Chorlton Road, going away to Brooks's Bar. The very left of the picture is in Stretford, and the far back of the picture is in Whalley Range, which gives an idea of how close these three areas are to each other. The large house on the right-hand side is the Seymour Hotel.

The Manchester Road just before its junction with Upper Chorlton Road, 1964. This is almost the same spot as above.

The Seymour Hotel on Upper Chorlton Road, looking from Seymour Grove, *c.* 1960. There is a zebra crossing across the bottom of Upper Chorlton Road. The Seymour started life as the home of Samuel Gratrix; both the end sections were added later when the house became an hotel. This corner is the subject of much misunderstanding, because Samuel's son (also called Samuel Gratrix) built a house on the opposite corner at the top of Seymour Grove. Therefore the Seymour is not the house that Charlie Peace tried to burgle (see p. 120).

Seymour Grove, Manchester 16, viewed from the car park of the Seymour Hotel, 1966. It was, I think, one Thomas Seymour who founded the firm of grocers, Seymour Meads, and who had the road, park and hotel named after him. How green the area looked.

Egerton Road from Upper Chorlton Road; this road was named after Wilbraham Egerton. The postcard was posted on 13 September 1932, but the photograph was taken in 1930. You will notice that the front of the card is marked Whalley Range, but Egerton Road is inside the Chorlton border even today.

Chorlton Road, 1913. We know this now as Upper Chorlton Road, and this photograph was taken from the corner where Egerton Road comes in: the long wall on the right can just be made out. The boundary between Chorlton and Stretford runs down the middle of the road, so technically these houses, including the bank and doctor's surgery, are in Stretford.

Clarendon Road, 1926. This lovely picture shows girls in school uniform, including hats, standing in the road opposite Manley Park, which is to the left of the picture.

West Point Corner, 1912. The photographer is standing on Seymour Grove corner and is looking down Manchester Road. An open-balcony tram is turning from Upper Chorlton Road and heading down Manchester Road. The Seymour Hotel (home of Sam Gratrix) is behind the wall at the back of the tram.

Above: Darley Hall, residence of Mr Reuben Spencer, who was one of the directors of John Rylands Limited, and took over the running of the company when John Rylands himself died in 1888. Darley Hall was built by Mr Wilson Crewdson and was noted for its Tudor style and large mullioned windows. The hall was built of stone and stood in 8 acres of ground, including a group of tall poplar trees noted for a rookery along Upper Chorlton Road. In 1902 it was recorded that there were 140 nests in these trees. The house was sold to Mr Jas. H. Dawson when Mr Spencer died in 1901, and became the subject of an early experiment of in garden city development. The buildings on Darley Hall grounds included the shops at West Point, Darley Road, Lindow Road and Chatham Road. The lessons learnt while building this estate were put to good use when building Chorltonville.

Left: Mr Reuben Spencer, owner and occupier of Darley Hall. He was born on 3 September 1830 and came to Manchester in 1846, taking up employment with John Rylands & Sons – where he worked his way up from the very bottom to become the employer of 12,000 people. Champion of the Manchester Ship Canal, magistrate, author, historian and devout churchman, he led by example, and his sudden death on 22 May 1901 was a great shock to those who knew him.

A very rare picture of West Point while Darley Hall was still there. Upper Chorlton Road goes away to the right and Seymour Grove to the left. The chimneys of Darley Hall can just be made out behind the trees on the left. A single-decker tram stands in Upper Chorlton Road, so the picture is later than 1903 but before 1908 when the shops started to be built. Mr Dawson, who purchased the Hall, allowed the front of it to be taken away and used in the construction of a Methodist chapel at All Saints, Chorlton-on-Medlock, where it stayed until the late 1960s.

Darley Road, Chorlton, showing the fine houses built by James Herbert Dawson and William John Vowles, c. 1907. A grass verge and trees segregate the footpath from the road, and the houses along the road all differ in design, an idea that was used again in the building of Chorltonville.

Wood Road, Whalley Range, says the caption on the front of this card, but the right-hand side of the road was in Chorlton. Down at the end of the road is the Lancashire Independent College, which was built in 1843 on land purchased from Samuel Brooks for £3,500. The 'Lancashire' as it was known was built by the Lancashire Union of Independent Churches, the Congregationalists, and trained preachers for missionary work all over the world. This beautifully situated seat of learning was always noted as an oasis of comfort in the south of Manchester. It is now the headquarters of the GMB Union, and is well maintained. A local resident who lived on Wood Road in a house called Claremont went on to fame and fortune. She was Dodie Smith, the writer of *One Hundred and One Dalmations* – which became a Walt Disney blockbuster. In her book *Look Back With Love*, Dodie Smith chronicled her schooldays and early life in Old Trafford and West Point.

Whalley Cottage stood on Upper Chorlton Road, on the corner of Egerton Road. It was built by the Gregory family and Mr Gregory, a solicitor, was the last occupant before it was demolished in 1964. Milton Lodge Flats now stand on this site.

The Lodge House which stood on the drive up to Manley Hall, 1912. After Manley Hall was demolished the drive became College Road, and the Lodge House was cleared away to make the road wider. Some say it had been the toll house where the charges put on Upper Chorlton Road, by Mr Brooks when it first opened were collected.

Upper Chorlton Road, looking towards Brooks' Bar, 1950. The tram lines have been cemented over, but the road is still cobbled with sets.

Bury Avenue. This road was built where Manley Hall once stood, and is reached via College Road, Park Drive and York Avenue. The postcard is one of a series from 1920, when travelling photographers would take shots of individual roads and then sell them at 6*d* per dozen to the occupants.

Whalley Range High School for Girls, *c.* 1900. Dodie Smith, author of *101 Dalmations*, was an old girl of the school, which stood on Withington Road, near College Road. It was very advanced for its time, being the first High School that specialised in girls' education, something that was not thought of as being that necessary in late Victorian times.

Pictures of shops with their staff outside were once very popular. This photograph of a shop on Upper Chorlton Road was no exception when it was taken in 1909. The shop today is still a baker and confectioner.

A rare photograph of Crimsworth House, which was just off Upper Chorlton near College Road. It was built by James Worrall in about 1885 as a family home. The name Crimsworth was taken from Crimsworth Dyeing Company, Hebden Bridge, Yorkshire, one of the first firms started by Mr Worrall. He also owned the dyeworks in Salford, and was for a time Mayor of Salford. All of this made his. embarrassment more pronounced when in 1890 his wife eloped with the curate of St Mary's on Upper Moss Lane. The scandal which rocked Victorian Chorlton was so immense that even *The Times* in London sent a correspondent hot-foot to Chorlton to cover the lurid story. Mr Worrall moved away, his sons took over the dyeworks, and the house became Crimsworth Kindergarten Teachers Training School, the very first of its kind in the country. In about 1969 Crimsworth House was demolished, and Manley Park Infant School was built on the site.

CHAPTER FOUR

CUM-HARDY

The name Chorlton-cum-Hardy, although quaint and old fashioned, does not go back that far. The fact that the name Chorlton has been around for almost 1,500 years, and Hardy for 1,000, would lead you to believe that they got together during the Norman period.

Looking very carefully at all the original manuscripts for the area, I cannot find any reference to Chorlton-cum-Hardy before 1700. When Chorlton was taken into the Poor Law Union that was being administered by Chorlton Row, in 1837, it was obvious that something had to be done about the names to avoid confusion. Chorlton Row became Chorlton-upon-Medlock, and Chorlton was referred to as Chorlton-cum-Hardy. Hardy Lane led to Hardy Farm, and that area was the small village of Hardy. Barlow Moor stretched from the Mersey Banks to Barlow Hall itself and was the biggest open area in the district.

Hardy's Lane, c. 1920. You can make out the houses of Chorltonville away in the distance to the left. The lane led from Hardy's Farm to what was then known as Jackson's Bridge.

Hardy's Farm, *c.* 1900. This lovely postcard dates from 1903, when you had to put your message on the front of the card, leaving the back for the address only. The public footpath down to the Mersey ran right through the farmyard and travellers would have had to run the gauntlet of any animals there. The farm was cleared away in about 1970 to make way for Manchester University sports buildings.

Hardy Lane, 1910: very much a rural backwater, leading down to Hardy Farm and with no sign of the council and private housing developement that was to follow. The photographer has managed to persuade a local girl to pose in her smock dress to complete the scene.

High Lane, Chorlton, *c.* 1910. This is what they mean by 'leafy suburbs'.

Nell Lane from the Clough, 1913. The hand-tinted card was printed in Saxony (soon to be an unpopular word, for it was part of Germany, and they were the enemy) for a series called 'Renaud' cards based in Chorlton, though I cannot find which newsagent was behind them. The Clough was where Wilbraham High School is today.

Chorlton Park, Manchester. This postcard was produced by A. Harold Clarke, Photographer, who had his premises at 83 Clarence Road, Chorlton. The park was only laid out in 1927 and opened in 1928 to give Chorltonians an open space amid the rapid development and building that seemed to be filling every corner of their village.

When Manchester took over the running of Chorlton in 1904 they promised that they would provide all the amenities that other areas closer to the city enjoyed. They were already supplying electricity (1902) and they took over the supply of gas from Stretford Gas Co. (1906); they began planting trees in 1908, trying to keep Chorlton looking a little rural. The first library followed in that same year, then war got in the way and everything was on hold. After the war Manchester promised two things for Chorlton, a properly laid-out park and public swimming baths, but it was 1928 before they got both of these. Here is the newly opened park with its freshly planted trees and shrubs and one of its main charms, an open-air theatre for band concerts, children's shows, contests, and other entertainment. Hundreds of wooden seats have been put out ready for its next use. Even today there always seems to be something going on in Chorlton Park, from football matches to visits from the travelling fair, and in recent years firework displays on bonfire night.

Keppel Road, 1909. The street name on the corner on the right says Stamford Road (named after the Earl of Stamford); the name is now Selborne Road, changed for some reason in the 1950s.

Keppel Road will go down in history for one thing only – the Bee Gees once lived there. Barry, Robin and Maurice Gibb were brought up in Chorlton and spent their early years here. I've seen books which say they were born in Australia (the family did emigrate there later) and the Isle of Man, but they lived in Keppel Road, Chorlton, and just recently a plaque was put on the house to prove it. Here we see a 1980 photo of, left to right, Maurice, Barry and Robin Gibb (photo *Manchester Evening News*).

Oak House Farm, from a charming card posted in August 1907. The farm was for many years the home of the Brundretts family who gave so much to the chapels of Chorlton. Brundretts Road is a memorial to that family. Where the farm was became the Shalimar cinema, and is now the drive-in for Kentucky Fried Chicken. The person (M.A.) sending the card refers to it as 'our place' and talks of being busy with harvest, hoping all will soon be safely gathered in.

High Lane, looking towards the Sandy Lane corner. The view is taken from a postcard issued locally in 1905, and shows a very select and quiet area.

Sandy Lane, once known as Moss Lane, and the corner with Barlow Moor Road, *c.* 1900. The white house was later used as a ticket and inspectors' office for the trams when they arrived here in 1911. Later the spot was a car sales area and then a tile showroom.

The shops on Sandy Lane on a postcard from the 'Renaud' series, 1908. It was used by A.H. Weller, who lived at No. 94, to thank Mrs Hunt for the lovely holiday they had just spent with her on Poplar Farm, Rowarth, near Stockport. They have obligingly marked the front of the card with an 'X' to show where they lived.

A wonderfully rural picture, taken from a creased hundred-year-old original, showing the River Mersey flowing gently past the inn that we call Jackson's Boat. The history of this establishment is buried deep in the mists of time and there are many variations on the theme. The place seemed to have started life as the Greyhound Inn, receiving its name from dogs that were kept and raced on the Eeys. There are many sports recorded for the area, including cock-fighting and badger-baiting, long after they had become illegal. The ease with which the felons could watch for 'peelers' from Lancashire, and then pop over the border into Cheshire, seemed to make this an ideal spot for nefarious activities.

Why this inn, which is south of the River Mersey, which means boundary, is under the jurisdiction of Chorlton at all is a bit of a mystery. Some say it is because a change in the river's path happened in the 1300s, but surely there would have been a change of boundaries since then. There was a ruling that if you built and maintained a bridge at your expense then the 100 yards either side of that bridge came under the authority of whoever paid for and maintained it. This happened in Stretford at the Crossford Bridge, with the Bridge Inn being in Lancashire though south of the river. Maybe that is what happened here, though the first bridge we have on record was here in 1816, built by Samuel Wilton, the owner of the inn, at a cost of £200. I wonder if it was the same Samuel Wilton who hedged in Chorlton Green: the dates fit. That bridge continued in use until December 1880, when a flood washed away the supports on the Chorlton side and made it unsafe.

Jackson's Boat, summer 1906. The river looks particularly subdued. The bridge, seen here from the Chorlton side, was built by landlord John Brooks in 1881 and opened with a celebration on 14 October that year. By a strange coincidence the old unsafe bridge was washed away in a flood the night before this bridge was opened.

Jackson's Footbridge, 1911. For some reason references to the earlier Jackson's Boat died away after the iron footbridge was built, and maps from the 1920s and '30s refer to the crossing as Jackson's Bridge. The pub has had a very good facelift in recent years and a pleasant evening in summer will find many people enjoying a pint in the beer garden at this lovely rural backwater.

A view of the inn and approach to the bridge, 1913. The caption refers to the Bridge Inn (Jackson's Boat), and the sign on the wall names the pub as the Bridge Inn. It is certain that the original Jackson was a landlord from the past, though records of him and details of his boat have been completely lost. There was a ferry here in 1800, which was propelled across the river by pulling on a chain that was anchored in each bank by a wooden post. When the first wooden bridge opened here the boat was placed outside the inn's entrance as an object of curiosity, and that may be where the references to Jackson's Boat came from. In 1982 the *Manchester Evening News* carried an article quoting Tom Gray, the landlord at the time, as very disappointed that Manchester City Council had turned down his request, backed by Trafford Council, for Jackson's Boat to be taken into Trafford. He was recorded as saying that he had been trying for the nine years he had been landlord and his predecessor had been trying for fifteen years before that. The 1982 report stated that Manchester wanted to settle all its boundary changes together, and promised that it would be sorted out by the Boundary Commission very shortly. If you take a look at the latest A-Z you will see that Jackson's Boat is still in the confines of Chorlton, even though the children's play area and gardens are in Trafford!

CHAPTER FIVE

CHORLTONVILLE

Most of those living in Chorlton today do not know or appreciate how much of a brave and social venture the building of Chorltonville was. James Herbert Dawson and William John Vowles came together through a Christian desire to better conditions for the working man of the day. It was these two individuals who pushed Manchester's councillors into making many building reforms. James Dawson had a brother-in-law, a New Zealander called Thomas Whiteley, who was a very capable builder. He built all the houses in the Corkland Road and Hartington Road area, and they stand today as witness to his fine workmanship. These three men banded together in 1910 to provide housing for the lower middle classes from the inner city area.

South Drive, Chorltonville, 1911. The concept of owning shares in the company that had built and managed your house was a novel one and newspapers of the day carried the story prominently. Postcard manufacturers from all over the country turned up to produce cards of Chorltonville. The delivery boy with his horse and trap add a nice touch to the scene.

Saturday 7 October 1911 was the day of the official opening ceremony for this new social experiment. Harry Nuttall, MP for Stretford, did the honours, supported by George Howarth JP and Dr Charles Leach, MP for the Colne Valley.

West Meade, Chorltonville, from a postcard issued by Barrett & Co., 40 Lancaster Avenue, Manchester, late 1920s. The hedges have grown by now and the trees are just developing. It was bright young architect Albert Cuneo who was engaged to prepare the plans for this 300-house garden village. No two adjacent pairs of semi-detached houses were to present the same front elevation, and Cuneo used designs and variations which were much copied for fifty years after.

A page from the brochure produced in 1912 to celebrate the opening of Chorltonville. Rents cost from £24 per annum, but people living on the estate were expected to take a strong interest in the running of the estate, with occupants expected to have at least two £5 shares in the company. The dividend from those shares was offset against the rent charged.

The Meade, 1914. The Meade was the centrepiece of the development and contained a large open grass area for children's play. It was James Dawson who came up with the specification that he wanted for his estate: 7 ft wide grass verges, 5 ft wide footpaths, 19 ft wide roads, to let taxis and delivery wagons pass. The roads when the estate first opened were made of crushed and compacted earth and gravel and were not tarmacked until much later. It was a private estate, so Manchester did not maintain the roads. The recreational side of life was not forgotten, and built into the estate were five tennis courts and a large bowling green.

Another page from the 1912 brochure celebrating the completion of the project. The text says it all: they wanted the hard-working, maybe lower middle-class man, to have and be able to afford a decent house and a chance in life for his family. The directors thought of everything for their residents, and even organised flower shows!

Our three heroes retired: Vowles to the hills of Wales, where he loved walking; Whiteley to a very quiet life in Cheshire; and Dawson to live beside the sea in the very sedate Lytham St Anne's. Our James was not the sort to sit back: the other two may not have been heard of again, but James was made of sterner stuff. He became a councillor so he could fight for a council that cared for its inhabitants. For thirty years he toiled as Head of the Education Committee, and eventually became mayor of Lytham St Anne's. James Herbert Dawson JP, FSMA, county councillor, alderman, church elder and man of the people passed away on 22 March 1963, aged ninety-five, and he was laid to rest in the cemetery at Lytham. It amazes me that there is no road named after this great man in the Chorlton area: it's something that should be rectified – and soon.

East Meade, from a 'Grosvenor' series postcard issued in 1912. The hedges are beginning to show behind the iron railings, the sapling trees have taken root and all the houses were soon occupied.

When our intrepid developers set out to build Chorltonville they had definite ideas in mind, but the Manchester Gas Co. said they would not provide gas for heating and cooking if the homes were not fitted with gas lights. The Electricity Board wanted to supply lighting and cooking, but cooking by electricity was not yet popular and the fight was a close-fought one. Gas won because people wanted, at the time, to cook by gas. When the houses where first occupied they had electric lights in the bedrooms and living rooms, but gas lights in the kitchen, scullery and wash-house at the back. The only thing that our directors failed to anticipate was the fact that the ordinary man would one day want to own a car of his own. Because public transport was so plentiful and there were lots of commercial firms that would provide transport for special occasions, they just did not foresee this as a possibility. There are no spaces for garages, drives, pull-ins, and all the other things that go with owning a car. That is the only fault I can see with the estate and I'm sure we can forgive its creators for that.

South Drive, Chorltonville, and a delivery boy poses happily with his handcart for this view, again from the 1912 'Grosvenor' series. The card was used by Ciss in September 1913 to thank her mum for the clothes and the shilling that she had sent. Young Ciss was staying with her aunt in Chorltonville and having a 'lovely time', pointing out to her mum that Auntie's house was on the card.

CHAPTER SIX

HALLS & HOUSES

For a small area, Chorlton-cum-Hardy has had more than its fair share of ancient halls and important houses. Even better is the fact that two of those ancient halls are still with us today: Barlow Hall, owned now by Manchester Corporation and in the very good stewardship of the Chorlton Golf Club, and Hough End Hall, which is older, and far too important historically to be pushed aside and left to get into a ruinous state. It would be nice if Manchester Council were to buy it and lease it out, to give the building more protection. Manley Hall, Hobson's Hall, Hardy Hall and very unfortunately Longford Hall have all gone, but in this book we attempt to catch a glimpse of the past of these once fine houses.

Barlow Hall, 1905. The water at the front of the hall was not the River Mersey but a fish pond that the Barlow family had constructed. The first hall was built on this spot in about 1290, but nothing of that original building remains today.

Barlow Hall, *c.* 1890. Some halls have one ghost but Barlow Hall has three. The ghost most seen is that of a lady, who lived in the hall during the late 1600s, and just why she has decided to hang around is the basis for many varied stories. Some of the older reports have her carrying her head around with her – as Stanley Holloway used to say, 'With her 'ead tucked underneath 'er arm'. That she is still there is not doubted. Staff at the golf club and customers enjoying an evening meal in the restaurant have seen her floating through the premises. Stories of sightings of ghosts at Barlow Hall have been around for years, and in the late 1700s one of the servants girls was so frightened by a young stable lad in a white sheet that she ran and threw herself in the river and drowned. Now she too can be seen, on clear moonlit nights, running down to the River Mersey to enact the scene all over again. There is also a male ghost, who is recorded as wearing yellow breeches. He is said to be very helpful, and will fetch and carry coal and other objects from room to room.

Barlow Hall as it was when Sir William Cunliffe Brooks lived there in 1890. The Barlow family died out in 1773, and the Egertons, who bought the property, rented the hall to some well-known inhabitants. One was Thomas Walker, the politician and reformer, who was also borough reeve of Manchester. The Walkers later bought Longford Farm (Hall), and they are the family who sold Longford to John Rylands. Sir William Cunliffe Brooks, the banker, lived at Barlow Hall for more than forty years, and would show antiquarian societies around the hall on great social evenings. He loved to tell stories of the Barlow family and the Hall's ghosts.

Barlow Hall as it appeared just after the golf club took over – a strange mixture of ivy-covered house, and newly erected sign for the parking of bicycles. The Barlow family came to the area in the 1200s from Barlow in Derbyshire, after one Alexander d'Albini settled some land he owned in the Hundred of Salford on Thomas de Barlow, after receiving considerable help from that gentleman. They settled on a payment of two pairs of white gloves each Christmas. It appears that they came to the area with the surname Barlow already, so this is one of the occasions where the family gave the name to the area, not the other way round.

The Hall was rebuilt almost completely in 1584, but a lot of that restoration was destroyed when it caught fire in March 1879 and the great hall and west wing were burnt out. The front of the house has seen two reconstructions since then, and now looks charming but plain. It has Grade Two listed status. A sundial dating from 1574 still remains.

The most famous Barlow is of course Ambrose Barlow, now at last St Ambrose Barlow. Born in November 1585 as Edward Barlow, he was the fourth son of Sir Alexander and Mary Barlow. He studied for the Church at Douay in France, then came back to England to face a life on the run, with the scaffold always a real threat. After spells in Lancaster Castle, he was hanged, drawn and quartered on Friday 10 September 1641, and as was the practice his body was put on display. His skull was spirited away by well-wishers and now rests at Wardley Hall, Salford, the home of the Roman Catholic Bishop of Salford. It is in a glass case built into the stairs, but is now minus the jaw-bone. That was given to the church of St Ambrose, Chorlton, which stands on Princess Parkway, in 1962. The Pope canonised Ambrose on 25 October 1970.

How different Ambrose's life was from that of his elder brother William. He too went to France to train as a Benedictine priest and took the name Father Rudesind. He wasn't sent back to England and lived to the age of seventy-two, becoming a venerated scholar and theology professor.

The west front of Barlow Hall, which today looks out over the golf course, 1904. With the death of Thomas Barlow in 1773, the Barlows died out altogether. Thomas's father, another Thomas, had died in Lancaster Castle of 'gaol fever', where he was 'resting' for trying to murder his wife. The last Thomas married a Miss Worral in 1760 but there were no sons to whom the Barlow estates could be passed, and in 1787, after years of wrangling, and after making sure Dame Barlow was looked after, the Hall and land were sold to the Egerton family – and the Barlows were no more.

Brookfield House, 1926. This house is situated inside Chorlton Park, and was taken over by Manchester Council when Chorlton Park was laid out and opened in 1928. It served as park-keepers' lodgings for many years, but was built as a private residence.

Hough End Hall, 1920s. This is Manchester's only remaining Elizabethan manor house, and the way it is put up for sale time after time is nothing short of scandalous. It is the oldest surviving complete house of its period inside the city of Manchester, yet it stands, as I write, up for sale again, after the last effort to revive it as a pub and restaurant failed. A monstrous tower block was built only 20 yards from the front door, and a school is less than 50 yards away. No venture can succeed here as parking, access and finding the place are now major problems. The Hall was built in about 1596 as a retirement home for Sir Nicholas Mosley after a life in London as a successful merchant, and Lord Mayor. He had helped Queen Elizabeth I over problems with the Spanish, and financed soldiers to stand at her side. There were Moseleys here in Chorlton before 1596, and it is said that Sir Nicholas had the Hall built on the site of an earlier house in which his father was born. It was also this Nicholas who dropped the middle 'e' from the family name and who bought the Manor of Manchester for £3,500 from John Lacey. Sir Nicholas died in December 1612, aged eighty-five, and the Hall then passed through various family members until it reached the hands of Lady Anne, who in 1685 married Sir John Bland in the chapel at Chorlton Green. John was not much good, and spent the family money and mortgaged the land: so bad was the situation that after the death of Lady Anne in 1734 the sons fell even further into debt, and the lands, which included much of Hulme as well as parts of Withington, were sold off to the Egertons and John Lloyd in 1751.

Hough End Hall, seen as a farm on a postcard from 1904. The Hall was rented from 1940 by Mr Leonard Bailey, who later bought the place. He tried very hard to get Manchester Council to buy it from him, but even when they bought a large piece of the land next to the Hall for a school, they would not take it as an administration block. After all the farmland had been sold off Councillor Bailey finally sold the Hall in 1950, as a hotel. He said it had been costing him £250 a year to keep it safe from vandals. The Baileys lived at Park Brow Farm on the corner of Sandy Lane and St Werburgh's Road. Mr Bailey was a Freeman of the City of London and held many other high positions.

Hough End Hall was still a farm in 1930, when this view was sold as postcard. The writer stated that she was staying at a house opposite the farm in the picture. It was known as Peacock Farm for many years, as the owner kept peacocks which strutted about outside. When the Egertons first purchased the Hall they took out the ancient staircase and moved it to Tatton Lodge, where it still is today.

Manley Hall, *c.* 1878. It was built by Sam Mendel, a merchant trader, in 1861. He was importing goods from the Far and Middle East, and making a lot of money from it. The Hall had greenhouses, orangery, deer park, fountains and ornamental lakes, and was built to the highest standards. Mendel went out of business when the Suez Canal opened, and had to sell the Hall to coal merchant Ellis Lever for £120,000 (which was never paid). The Manley Hall Winter Garden Society Ltd was formed by a London estate agent called Fuller, but this turned out to be a scheme to part people from their money, and it put the fate of the Hall in doubt. From 1875 the house was opened at weekends and in summer, and people enjoyed the beautiful gardens and fine amenities – but this only lasted five years, and in January 1879 the company leasing the Hall was wound up.

Manley Hall, *c.* 1905: boarded up, grounds in need of care, greenhouses gone, and just waiting to be pulled down. There had been various schemes to revive the Hall, but all fell through. Parts of the grounds became a golf course for the Manchester Golf Club, and other plots were sold off for housing, as people found Chorlton a convenient place to live. Manchester Council did not want to pay for the Hall as they felt they had enough parks and open spaces already. Sam Mendel never recovered and died in poverty on 17 September 1894. The Hall was finally pulled down in 1912, and what was left of the gardens became a small park, which is still there today.

Northleigh House, which stood on the south side of the junction of Seymour Grove and Manchester Road, facing Upper Chorlton Road. This was the house built by Sam Gratrix the younger, which faced his father's house (later The Seymour Hotel). It was this house that Charlie Peace, the murderer, was trying to break into when he was disturbed. This photograph shows the house in the 1960s when it was a home for retired licensed victuallers, and residents are enjoying a game of bowls on the green which stood on the far side of the house, away from the road. The row of shops on Upper Chorlton Road are on the right of this photograph. This large house was pulled down during the 1970s, and sheltered housing was built on the site.

A rare view of the inside of Darley Hall, which stood where Darley Road, off Seymour Grove, is today. This picture shows the top of the main hallway, and was taken just before the Hall was pulled down. There are obvious signs of decay and neglect. Nevertheless, the photograph shows what a grand house it was.

The Lancashire Independent College, as it appeared in all its glory on a 1912 postcard. Independent was another term for the Congregational Church movement, and pupils would go out practising their sermons in chapels all over Lancashire and Cheshire when the pastors were on holiday or indisposed. The foundation stone was laid on 23 September 1840, and on that day the stand bearing ladies watching the proceedings collapsed. Fortunately, there were only bruises and broken bones.

Luckily, when the college closed it was taken over by the GMBU. The union have kept the hall in fine condition and it is always busy with seminars, meetings and what it was intended for – spreading knowledge among the people.

Stretford Memorial Hospital. AHC.1273.

Basford House, or, as the caption says, Stretford Memorial Hospital. As part of the plans to remember those who gave their lives during the First World War, this building was turned into a Cottage Hospital for Stretford and Old Trafford. There were a children's ward, a maternity unit and a geriatric ward, and it served the community very well; it still does. This building has another claim to fame. In 1892, in the coachhouse that was attached to the house, was born one John William Alcock, who in June 1919 became the first man to pilot a plane across the Atlantic Ocean. There is a plaque on the building to record the fact, though it says he was born in the house – and his birth certificate says he was born in the lodge, where his father worked as a coachman.

Spout Hall, Chorlton. I know it's not an ancient hall, but Cosgrove Hall has become very important in the area. Situated at the top of Albany Road, off Brantingham Road, the firm, which devises and produces cartoons and cartoon characters, has grown in popularity and is now well known all over the world. It first came to my attention when I was watching with my youngsters a cartoon programme called *Chorlton and the Wheelies*, which was made for Thames Television in the late 1970s. It was a great series, and was narrated by Brian Trueman, well known in television circles. The 'happiness dragon' called Chorlton spread smiles and laughter wherever he went, and appealed to all ages. Fenella, the wicked witch, tried every week to dampen his spirits with an evil spell, but fifteen minutes later the 'happiness' had broken out again and all was well around Chorlton. The company is very successful, and has produced other successful characters such as Count Duckula and produced such fine work as *Toad of Toad Hall*.

Our photo shows the famous Chorlton himself with Fenella on his right, surrounded by Wheelies, with Spout Hall, that's the kettle where Fenella lived, behind. They say that Chorlton still resides at Cosgrove Hall and every now and again shakes some happiness dust into the air to settle over Chorlton – usually at about 10 o'clock on a Friday evening (photo: Pearson Television).

CHAPTER SEVEN

CHURCHES & CHAPELS

Chorlton-cum-Hardy has more than its fair share of churches and chapels, and could have been regarded as something of a hot-bed of Nonconformism a century and a half ago. It was the Barlows who paid for the first chapel of ease to be built on common land, by The Green. They also paid for the church, built in about 1512 on the same spot, but when Henry VIII broke away from the Church of Rome they did not, and were noted followers of the 'Old Faith'. Eventually the power of the district moved to the Mosleys when they arrived. They supported the new faith, and were great protagonists in the fight against Catholicism. In 1967 the Chorlton-cum-Hardy Fellowship of Churches was formed, and now the chapels and churches work together to help the community, and keep alive the spirit of Christian friendship.

The old parish church of St Clement, Chorlton Green, c. 1901. In the foreground children stand next to a gaslight, which was placed where the bull-baiting stone used to stand. The lamp was moved to The Green soon after this view was taken. The first chapel was in a very poor state by 1779 when a start was made on the church seen here. The church was enlarged in 1837 and again in 1893, but as the centre of Chorlton moved the church became out of the way, and was not convenient for the new parishioners.

A very rare photograph of the interior of the old parish church of St Clement's, *c.* 1889. The church became a parish church in 1839 and served well until Wilbraham Road was cut and houses started to be built at Martledge. This church would have been swept away in the 1860s except for the strong support given by a few very influential and powerful men who caused the new church to take a back seat to the old parish church. One little recorded fact is that in 1782 the stipendiary curate here was one Joshua Brooks, an eccentric character, who is forever etched into the history of the area by appearing in the book *The Manchester Man.* Mr Brooks became perpetual curate in 1789 but resigned in 1791 on being appointed to the Collegiate Church in Manchester. Apparently he would finish the service on Sunday, rush to Stretford to stand by the Bridgwater canal and hitch a lift back into Manchester where he often stayed. The fine stained glass east window behind the altar was given to the church by Sir William Cunliffe Brooks. The church was more or less redundant during the war years, and was closed in 1940 when frost damage proved too dear to repair. It was pulled down in 1949, leaving behind the garden and gravestones we see today.

Ninety years ago there was a strange state of affairs in Chorlton. There were three memorial churches in one small area, all dedicated by different branches of the Methodist faith to three different preachers. All these preachers were Scottish and all had names beginning with Mc or Mac: the McLaren Memorial Baptist Church, which stood on Wilbraham and Sibson Road corner; the Macfadyen Memorial Congregational Church on Barlow Moor Road; and the Macpherson Primitive Methodist Church on High Lane.

St Clement's new church, *c.* 1905. This church had a lot of problems in its early life. The plans to build it were first formulated in 1860 when Lord Egerton offered land at Pingot Hey, the corner of Edge Lane and St Clement's Road. One stipulation was that the parish church and his endowment would be transferred to the new church when completed. When that could not be promised, all work on the new church, designed by Pennington & Brigden, stopped. The money for the church then had to come from the new Chorltonians who were moving into the Wilbraham Road area, and this was slow in coming forth. A foundation stone was never formally laid, and the building was stop-start, completion of the first part of the church taking over six years. Even when it did open on Saturday 23 June 1866 it was licensed for Divine Service only and not for weddings. The church remained technically a chapel of ease as long as the 'old church' was there.

St Clement's Church, on the corner of St Clement's Road and Edge Lane, in a fine view from local photographer A. Harold Clarke, 1920s. After the church opened in 1866 work carried on, and the vestry and north transept were added in 1883. In July 1895 the very first formal ceremony took place, when the foundation stone of the south transept was laid with full masonic honours; when this opened in 1896, to a design by W. Higginbottom, the church was consecrated, and stopped paying 10*s* a year ground rent to the Egertons. The church became the parish church in 1940, and in 1977 underwent a major refit to give extra meeting rooms, a hall and a kitchen, which are much appreciated today when the church plays host to various organisations, drop-ins, and functions. St Clement's is a busy church that is providing a caring heart for the community around it.

Parish Church.   Chorlton-Cum-Hardy.

This postcard from about 1904 is an example of what happened when an outside photographer went into an area he did not know well, spent a day taking photographs, then produced postcards for the area – printed far away in Saxony for cheapness. The words on the front say 'Parish Church', but as we know the old church was still standing and was officially the parish church. The church dedication isn't given either – but it must have been confusing to have had two churches, both called St Clement's and one at either end of St Clement's Road, named after the 'old church', which was by then tucked away behind The Green.

A close-up view of the Macfadyen Memorial Church which stood in Barlow Moor Road. It was the Rev. Mr Macfadyen who obtained permission from the Masonic authorities to hold a service in the Masonic Hall on High Lane on 29 September 1879. People continued to meet there until a school and church had been built on the corner of Zetland Road: it is still there today.

When houses started to be built near the new Chorlton railway station and Egerton Road South was being developed, it was felt that a new church was needed, and St Werburgh's parish was created in 1898. St Werburgh's shrine was at Chester and the cathedral there was formerly, until 1540, the Benedictine Abbey of St Werburgh, so in late Victorian times many people looked upon this good lady as Patron Saint of Cheshire; this may have led to the dedication. The foundation stone was laid on 29 September 1899 by Lord Wilbraham Egerton of Tatton, though services were already taking place in a temporary iron building that also housed a Sunday school. The chancel and transepts were dedicated on 28 September 1900 and the church opened fully on 1 June 1902. *Right*: An invitation to the church's formal consecration, St Swithun's Day, 1902. I wonder why they didn't wait for St Werburgh's Day, though I suspect they thought it might have been too cold on 3 February. (Werbergh herself lived from about AD 640 until 705, and was the daughter of the first Christian king of Mercia.) The Lord Bishop of Manchester who preached the sermon was Bishop James Moorhouse, who before becoming Bishop of Manchester had been Bishop of Melbourne, Australia.

Church of S. Werburgh,
CHORLTON-CUM-HARDY.

CONSECRATION
At 7-30 p.m. on
S. Swithun's Day *(Tuesday, July 15th),*
1902.
SERMON by the Right Reverend The
Lord Bishop of Manchester.

The Clergy are requested to bring Cassock, Surplice, and Hood.

Coffee in the Hall (adjoining the Church) after Service.

R.S.V.P. TO REV. GEORGE J. LOVETT,
49, WILBRAHAM ROAD,
CHORLTON-CUM-HARDY.

The Roman Catholic parish made its first appearance at The Priory, which once stood where Priory Road and Needham Avenue are today. The building, formerly called Oakley, had been erected in 1835 but was sold to the church by a Mr Needham in 1890, when Bishop Vaughan started a parish in Chorlton. Benedictine priests led by the Bishop's brother, Father Jerome Vaughan, came from Scotland to minister to the 120 Catholics who lived in the area. The parish was originally called St Augustine's, and after the Benedictines had established it they moved on, leaving a building on High Lane as the church, with a presbytery next door and a schoolroom behind.

The church of Our Lady and St John, which stands on High Lane. In 1916 Father Joseph Kelly took over the parish and a great push was made towards a more fitting church for Chorlton. In 1925 Father Kelly bought the church of St Andrew's in Ramsbottom, intending to move it stone by stone to Chorlton, and as Mary and John Leeming had agreed to pay the bill, the new church was going to be named Our Lady and St John to remember them. In the end only the pews and fittings came to High Lane; the spire ended up on English Martyrs church on Alexandra Road South. The new red brick and yellow terracotta church opened in June 1927, and the new title of the parish was confirmed. Monsignor Kelly died in 1930, and his successor, who led his congregation through the Second World War, was Canon Edward McGuinness, who died in 1946. The Barlow family practised the Catholic faith during the years when Henry VIII was busy stamping it out. They had a chapel in Barlow Hall, where they held secret masses up until the middle of the eighteenth century.

Beech Road chapel, decorated for a harvest festival, *c.* 1880. They say that Methodism in Chorlton began in 1770, when a soldier in a red coat who had walked from Manchester decided to give an impromptu sermon on Chorlton Green. After this there were meetings in people's homes and even in a barn until a church was built in 1805, on Beech Road. The chapel we see here was the second Wesleyan one in Beech Road, built in 1827 and originally much taller than the building still standing today. When it opened there was segregation inside, with men on the right and the fairer sex on the other. Note the crude benches, covered, it appears, with carpet for comfort. Jeremiah Brundrett, father and son, had helped pay for this chapel to be built, and it served for many years.

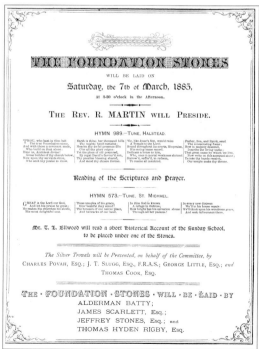

A page from the brochure which accompanied the laying of the foundation stones for the new Sunday school on Manchester Road, 7 March 1885. Pupils had been taught in the chapel in Beech Road since July 1873, when the new church on Manchester Road opened, but their numbers increased from 80 in 1865 to 318 on the roll at the time the foundation stones were laid.

Another picture of the inside of the old Wesleyan Methodist chapel on Beech Road decorated for a harvest festival. These are early photographs, there is no doubt about that, but the year was not recorded. The new church on Manchester Road had been built by 1873, and it seems that this old chapel became just the Sunday school until 1886, so are these celebrations for the Sunday school? There was a bad fire on 21 November 1883, so did the congregation revert to the old chapel while the church was being restored?

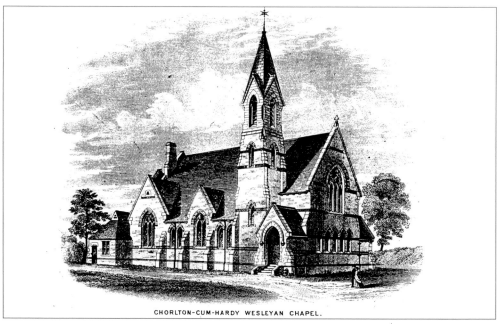

CHORLTON-CUM-HARDY WESLEYAN CHAPEL.

A drawing of the new Manchester Road Wesleyan Methodist church, as it would have been when it opened on 2 July 1873. The land had been bought from Lord Egerton in 1871 at a chief rent of 2*d* per square yard, and building had commenced almost straight away. After the fire in 1883 work began on the Sunday school. The church is still there and busier than ever with 'good neighbours' and Visiting schemes. It was one of the founder churches in the Chorlton Fellowship of Churches in 1967.

Barlow Moor Road, 1904, showing a very rural scene dominated by the newly completed Macfadyen Memorial Congregational church. James (Anglicised to John) Macfadyen was born at Greenock and soon received the calling to join the Congregational, or Independent, movement. He studied at the Lancashire Independent College on the Chorlton/Whalley Range border, and it was the happy time spent learning the Bible and forming his spiritual life in this part of the world that led to him taking up the post of preacher to Chorlton Road Congregational chapel in 1863. He led by example, and many churches all over the world tried to tempt him to become their minister, but he stayed in south Manchester. When Macfadyen died in 1890 his death was mourned by all branches of the Christian Church: he was a truly great man.

The Macfadyen Memorial church, 1920s. The cornerstone of the church was laid on 16 September 1893 by Mr Macfadyen's widow and the church opened for public worship on 25 October 1894. The first building to be completed on the site was a school and meeting room on the corner of Holland Road. When the church was pulled down in 1974 the congregation reverted, once again, to the meeting rooms, still standing today. In 1972 they merged with the Presbyterian Church to become the United Reformed Church. In October 1975 the building was home to the Chorlton central church, and is still a focal point in community life.

The Manley Park Methodist church, a 'tin tabernacle' which stood on the corner of Clarendon Road and Cromwell Avenue, 1904. It was looked after by a retired minister and had always to share its ministers with other duties. The postcard, postmarked 31 July 1904, includes 'our Eddie' says the writing on the back.

A new chapel was built on the opposite corner to the one above, and though the date above it says 1909, that actually records when the work was started; it didn't open until 1910. The postcard from 1920 shows the Manley Park Wesleyan Methodist chapel on Egerton Road in fine fettle. The church is still there today, and seems to have won its battle with dry rot. For a while trainee ministers from Hartley Victoria College would gain preaching experience by taking the Sunday morning service here.

The Unitarian Church, c. 1920. The church, which stood on Wilbraham Road near to its junction with Edge Lane, was opened on 9 February 1901 and had a strong following. It looked just like a country chapel, with its black and white woodwork, and when it opened there was still quite a bit of open land around it.

The Unitarian church, just off Wilbraham Road, as it was being demolished in the late 1970s. The wooden church served the community well and was a polling station for some years. In the end dry rot was its downfall, though its message stood out to the very last.

St Barnabas's Church, which stands on Hardy Lane, was built in 1951 to serve the south of the district and to replace the old parish church of St Clement's on Chorlton Green, which had closed during the Second World War and was finally pulled down in 1949. A brick building, it is now twinned with the new parish church of St Clement's.

Barlow Moor Methodist church, as it stands today on Maitland Road. Opened in 1932 and once a busy and bustling place, it now seems to have been abandoned, with the minister's name painted out and the gates firmly locked.

CHAPTER EIGHT

TRANSPORT

Travelling was not easy for the ordinary person of ancient Chorlton. The upper classes had their carriages and coachmen, but for the peasants from the farms of Chorlton it was an adventure to walk into Manchester to see the 'goings-on' at the fair on St Matthew's Day. When the Duke of Bridgewater's Canal arrived in Stretford in 1780, it was still a mile walk, then a barge ride into town, and at 1*d* a mile the money could be better spent. When the Altrincham and South Junction Railway opened its station at Stretford it started the development of large houses on Edge Lane towards Chorlton.

A horse and coach waiting in what was then Manchester Road opposite St Clement's Church, c. 1904. The card was made by 'postcard makers to her late Majesty Queen Victoria', A. & G. Taylor of London, and whoever they sent to take the photograph had a knack for collecting local children to pose for the picture. There are about thirty of them included, and they would all be over ninety if alive today.

The first horse omnibuses in the area were private concerns. Here an open-topped horse bus is drawn up at Chorlton Green. The horse buses ran from 1880, while the Horse and Jockey has not yet received its black and white façade, so the photograph was taken before 1905, when this hand-tinted card was postmarked. Horse buses finished in Manchester in 1902, but The Green only became public property again in 1897. This is probably a 'Sunday Special' service of buses from Manchester to Chorlton Green over a hundred years ago, and perhaps it was the special occasion that prompted the photographer to take the picture.

To get an alcoholic drink on a Sunday you had to be a bona fide traveller, and the law stated that you had to travel 3 miles to qualify as such. Chorlton was just 3 miles from the centre of Manchester, and we find in 1864 one Christopher Batty running Sunday horse buses to Chorlton Green 'to sample the delights of the countryside and enjoy drinking as a bona-fide traveller'. They were popular too: in the summer the whole family could go, after church of course, for a few coppers.

According to the original caption, this single-decker tram is standing at West Point after a journey from Manchester via Brooks' Bar. It is obviously a posed picture as the connecting bar to the electricity always pointed to the back of the tram, and this one is ready to go back. The destination board says Seymour Grove, and that was where the end of the line was when the very first tram made its way down Chorlton Road on 13 April 1903. The wall to the left was the boundary wall of the Darley Hall estate.

An open-ended double-decker tram passes Kemp's druggist shop on Barlow Moor Road, c. 1914. The first tram operators thought there was no need to come right into Chorlton as it was served by the railway, but they soon found that people were getting lazy and wanted to get on public transport as near as possible to their front doors. The line to Upper Chorlton Road was extended to run right through 'new' Chorlton in 1907, and the first tram ran across Wilbraham Road and down to High Lane on 7 May 1907.

An open-topped tram waits at the end of the line, probably 1907. The end of the line at that time was the High Lane/Barlow Moor Road corner, and Sandy Lane can be seen going off to the right. Trams were open topped when first introduced, not for the love of fresh air but because the operators thought they would topple over in high winds if the upper deck was enclosed. Trams arrived here, from West Point, on 7 May 1907, and from the number of onlookers the novelty still hadn't worn off at the time of this photograph.

The No. 22 tram from Moston to Chorlton rests at Chorlton Office, the tram terminus that opened to traffic on 24 May 1915. The line to Southern Cemetery had been introduced from High Lane on 31 May 1911, and when the tram line from town to Alexandra Park was extended to Chorlton in 1913 the twin tracks at High Lane and Barlow Moor Road just couldn't cope with the terminating traffic – so the tram terminus was opened.

The bus terminal from the corner of Beech Road, 1950. Though the trams and the overhead wires have gone, the tram lines (and cobbles) running through the terminus can still be seen. The Macfadyen church is still there, and the roads and pavements seem remarkably clutter-free.

The same view as above, 1960s. Bollards have been introduced on Beech Road corner and there is a police motor-scooter parked outside the police station. 'Edie' used the card to write home to his or her folks in Scotland, telling them he/she was well, studying hard and living in Chorlton. At least one of the private houses opposite the terminus must have taken in lodgers in the late 1960s – handy for the bus at least.

A view of Chorlton railway station, from a Thornton postcard posted in 1909, though the view is at least five years earlier. The small building at the front is a goods office, and the main station is the longer apex-roofed building behind. The Midland Railway was determined to get a route into Manchester and open a goods terminal there. The companies that had built the existing lines into Manchester either didn't allow the Midland to run over their rails or charged so much that it wasn't economical. There was talk of a joint effort, with the Midland involved, to build a new railway into Manchester, but the other parties, Great Northern & Great Central, seemed to be dragging their feet. The Midland Railway bought land and laid the lines from Throstles Nest junction at Old Trafford to Heaton Mersey, and then built Chorlton station. It was a typical Midland Railway station, similar to others all over the system. The stations at Fallowfield and Wilbraham Road built later by the Cheshire Lines Committee were different and not as ornate.

Engine No. 41072 LMS 4–4–0 3-cylinder Compound brings a local stopper from Manchester to rest in Chorlton station on 14 September 1954. Trains ran from Manchester Central, through here and on to Stockport's Tiviot Dale station on the original 1880 line, and through Fallowfield and Hyde Road stations on the line added in 1991 (Locofotos).

An early and very heavily re-touched photograph of Chorlton railway station. The footbridge, which dominates the picture, didn't last long; it was taken away during the First World War, to save money on repairing and maintaining it. After that passengers had to use the road bridge to change platforms. From opening, on 1 January 1880, the station was a busy one, over 200 season tickets for Manchester being sold in the first month. You could be in Manchester in seven minutes, while some middle management even came home for their lunch on the train. A hundred years ago you would have paid 5*d* for a return third-class ticket to town, and the same for a first-class single. There were more than fifty trains a day each way, the first to Manchester at 6.36 a.m., and the last home at 11.17 p.m.

Eastern Region 2–6–4 No. 67747 (L1 class) guides a stopping train heading for Sheffield (Midland) station, into Chorlton station on 20 June 1959. The line through Dinting and Woodhead to Sheffield was opened by the Great Central Railway from Chorlton Junction on 1 October 1891 and the stations at Wilbraham Road and Fallowfield at the same time. The running of the Chorlton section of the line was transferred to the Cheshire Lines Committee, and it stayed that way until Nationalisation (W. Brown).

LMS tank engine No. 42676 pulling into Chorlton railway station with a rush-hour evening stopping train from Manchester Central, 14 September 1954. The station closed on 1 January 1967 and was cleared away soon after. A single line was left, to be used for freight workings that missed out the city centre and for the odd diverted passenger train. Right up until the early 1990s the line was used by goods trains only, pulled by heavy steam engines at first, and later by Deltic diesels. (Locofotos)

Standard engine No. 73000 pulls into Chorlton, late 1950s. These 4–6–0 engines weren't introduced until 1951, and didn't have a very long working life before being scrapped. The sidings that stood on the Albany Road side of the station can just be seen. There was a pick-up goods arrangement from Chorlton for many years: parcels were loaded into a goods van all day, and this was taken away at tea time for sorting at the railway warehouse on Deansgate.

CHAPTER NINE

THE CHANGING FACE OF CHORLTON

Chorlton has been changing since early in the last century. One hundred and fifty years ago it was just starting to grow and develop, because of the arrival of the railway at Stretford and the cutting of the new (Wilbraham) Road. Since then it has gone from the place for the top echelons of society to the place for middle-class (though slightly upper middle-class) man to today's mixture, with students and ageing hippies among the multi-faceted community. Buildings change their uses, grand houses become flats, and blocks of shops change their public face overnight. In an age when charity shops and banks seem to be the only solid thing in society, we look at some of the more recent changes in Chorlton-cum-Hardy.

Chorlton shopping precinct, with its welcoming group of shops.

The Oaks Hotel, which stood facing Southern Cemetery at the end of Barlow Moor Road. It was a big pub, and being positioned where it was it got a lot of people dropping in after a funeral. At least half the drinkers there on a normal weekday would be wearing black ties. I went in there about eight times and only once was it not for a funeral. The place was boarded up in the early 1990s and pulled down shortly afterwards.

In the 1960s it had been known as the Princess Club, and many of the top names in entertainment could be seen there. I've seen The Drifters, Bob Monkhouse, Billy J. Kramer, Lonnie Donegan and Tom Jones, to name but a few. The 1980s were not kind to the place and it changed its name, and its markets, a few times, ending as Ra Ra's Showbar – seen here being boarded up.

They really did try everything with this place before it was put up for sale for re-development – Adam & Eve's Discotheque, Valentine's Health Club, Charlie Brown's Fun Pub – but people had just got out of the habit of a good night out: video had arrived.

The same spot as above but just eighteen months later. It didn't take long once they started on the old club. With McDonalds' money behind the project it was soon completed, and we have, as we still do today, a drive through burger take-away and restaurant.

The Mersey Hotel on Princess Parkway was a very famous place in the 1960s. People came from all over south Lancashire and north Cheshire to bop the night away. Many famous names cut their teeth here, and it was one of the leading pubs (it was almost considered a club) in Manchester. Little and Large, Bernard Manning, Les Dawson, Freddie and the Dreamers: the list of people who regularly appeared here is almost endless. You would get a compere, a comedian, a singer or group, and sometimes a speciality act as well. Not bad for just the price of your ale. Our photo shows the place billed as the Mersey Lights, and boarded up just before its demolition to make way for a petrol station.

The cover of a brochure advertising the highlights showing at the Shalimar Cinema, Chorlton, August 1980. Actually the cinema looked nothing like the illustration on the cover, but it was probably the only block the printers had of a cinema. *The Life of Brian*, *The Black Hole*, and *The Love Bug* were among the attractions tempting young Chorltonians in the summer of 1980. The cinema later became a bicycle store and was cleared away a few years ago to make way for Kentucky Fried Chicken.

Chorlton baths opened on 19 September 1929, as part of a campaign to make a 'Healthier Manchester'. Mixed bathing was permitted from the outset – an advanced notion! *Below*: the baths are seen as they were on opening.

Chorlton Water Park came about because earth was needed to build up the new motorway that was being constructed around Manchester. It is now twenty-five years since it was created, and it has proved a real blessing to the area for the recreation facilities it provides, as well as being an important and much-needed nature reserve. The Park is well maintained by the Park Rangers, who also arrange plenty of outdoor activities for anyone interested in the countryside, or in the wide variety of wildlife that exists here. Our autumnal view shows the water park from the motorway end. The lake is exactly a mile long, a boon I'm told for runners and joggers.

Feeding the ducks, geese and swans is a pleasant task, and passes an hour or so at the weekend. This is your author, compiler and guide, enjoying the benefits of the peace of Chorlton Water Park, with the highlight of my life, granddaughter Hannah, aged nine months.

CHAPTER TEN

POSTSCRIPT

A multi-view card of Chorlton, 1930s, posted in December 1939, just after the outbreak of war. As can be expected for a card sent in 1939 it wishes the best for Christmas and that 'The New Year ushers in sight of the Peace we all hope for'. We know different now, don't we?

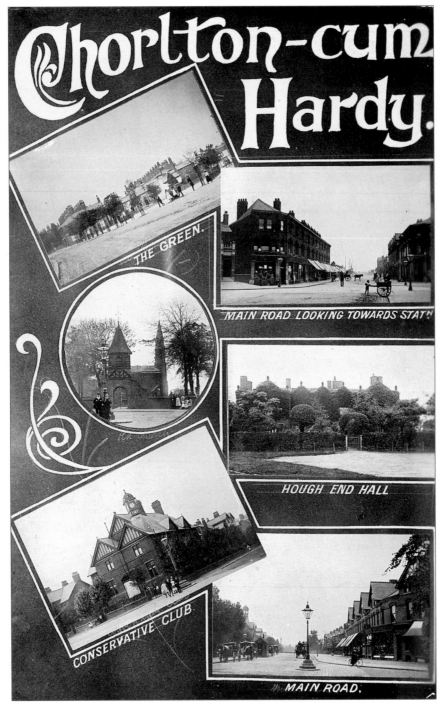

A multi-view card, 1905. It's strange that all the views have a caption except the round one, and that two views of Wilbraham Road are marked Main Road. Maybe there was still doubt over the name of the road, or maybe it was one of the travelling postcard photographers. It must have been frustrating for them to capture on film (and in one day) an area they knew nothing about. Hough End Hall still has the gates that marked its life as a farm, and the round picture is the church down below Chorlton Green.

A multi-view card from the postcard firm Valentine's, late 1950s. Local historians can be grateful that Valentine's sent out agents to sign up local newsagents, and produced these multiview cards until the 1970s. The views would have also been produced as single postcards, but these are harder to find these days, and more expensive. Top left is the Wilbraham/Barlow Moor Road corner looking towards Stretford. On the right is the view from outside the post office looking left. In the centre is Chorlton Park, while below is the cinema in its Gaumont days and right, further down Barlow Moor Road.

Recently I came across a bundle of postcards marked BBC. They were all addressed to Jim Dale, Children's Favourites, BBC, and were all view cards of the 1960s. From the markings it is clear that Deborah got her request played on 19 June 1966. But who saved the cards and how did they make their way back to Chorlton?

I do not know of anywhere else in the Manchester area where there is a wall across the road. Not a wall with a gate or a doorway in it, but a brick wall across a continuous road. This is the top of Grange Road in Chorlton, where the wall marks the boundary between Chorlton, Manchester and Firswood, Stretford, Trafford. The other side of the wall is Edward Charlton Road, named after a local man who won the VC in the Second World War, but why the wall? It protects the back gate of St Hilda's Junior School from passing traffic, and it stops a peaceful area from being just another cut-through, but this doesn't fully explain it. Manchester Council tell me that the wall has been renewed and rebuilt in recent years. I would love to know why it went up, and why there isn't at least a doorway in it.

A busy view outside the gates of Southern Cemetery, 1915. The No. 46 passes the No. 45, both heading for Piccadilly but each taking a different route. It was on 31 June 1911 that the tramlines were extended from here to West Didsbury and that opened the way for a lot more tram traffic to pass through Chorlton. The cyclist in our picture has his hands full steering his way through the mass of carriages, trams and hearses. The last tram trundled through Chorlton on 22 November 1942. It should have been much earlier but the withdrawal of services that had begun in March 1938, with the No. 31 service from Fairfield converting to a bus, were stopped when war came along, and some tram services were reinstated to save petrol. The No. 38 service from Albert Square last ran on 3 September 1938, and the No. 22 from Moston Cemetery also ran for the last time in that year.

Manchester United often used the Hough End playing fields as a training ground. Here we see a young Matt Busby meeting his players for the first time after joining Manchester United as their manager in 1946. Matt is shaking hands with Johnny Carey, and Tony Dowe, John Hanlon, Allenby Chilton, Stan Pearson, John Ashton and others look on.

Matt Busby at his home in King's Road, Chorlton, pictured with the Central League Trophy that United Reserves won in the 1955/6 season. It must be nice when you can take home the silverwear to brighten up the sideboard. Sir Matt is still here in Chorlton, resting peacefully alongside his wife Jean in Southern Cemetery.

Sir Robert Mark was once the most famous policeman in the land. He was born in Chorlton in March 1917, at a house in Clarendon Road West, where he lived with his parents until he was ten. He attended Manley Park Elementary School, which he remembers was made of tin. The family later moved to Tintern Lodge, on the Upper Chorlton Road/Seymour Grove corner, and in his autobiography he tells that it was the wall of this house that had the famous bullet mark from the gun of Charlie Peace. He joined the Manchester Police Force in July 1937 and worked his way up, finishing as Metropolitan Commissioner of Police. On his retirement from the Met he turned down the job of head of Australia's Police Force and settled down to write his life story, *In the Office of Constable*, which was published in October 1978. As part of the publicity he came back to Manchester, and is seen here being shown round Mill Street police station where he was once a young copper. Sir Robert lived in Daventry Road, Chorlton, with his wife right up to the time of his appointment as Chief Constable of Leicester (*Manchester Evening News*).

THE STORY OF CHARLIE PEACE

Charles Peace was a villain, of that there is no doubt. There have been many articles, books, and magazine articles written about Mr Peace, and most of them show a different man, or at least a different side of him – and this is the only photograph in existence. Born in Sheffield in 1832, son of an animal trainer, he would have spent his early years around wild and large animals. As a young boy he had an accident while working in a mill, and it left his hand twisted and not much use. How strong Charlie's connections with Chorlton were is hard to judge. He liked to play the fiddle outside large houses while casing them ready to burgle when the coast was clear, and Chorlton was full of houses like this. He was arrested and sent to jail at Stretford for burglary, his second visit to jail, and while in there he had another accident. I think some other inmates tried to hang Charlie; whatever happened he came out with a scar round his neck and a promise never to get caught again. Local folk legend says that Charlie was a regular drinker in the Royal Oak in Chorlton. Some years ago I was told the story of an old barber's shop on Chester Road, Stretford, which had the name C. Peace etched into the window glass, made as Charlie proved that a ring he had stolen was a genuine diamond.

On the night of 2 August 1876 Charles Peace was in Chorlton, near the Chorlton Road/Manchester Road junction. He was caught coming out of a large house there, and when PC Nicholas Cock told him to halt, he opened fire with the gun he kept strapped to his 'poor' hand.

PC Nicholas Cock, a 5 ft 7 in copper, who had been in the Lancashire Police Force, died less than a year later. Because PC Cock had given local Irish immigrant workers such a hard time, suspicion fell on the three Habron brothers, who were arrested, and on very flimsy evidence William Habron was sentenced to hang. The sentence was changed to life as William was only eighteen years old.

Charlie went on to other murders, and when sitting in Armley Prison awaiting execution he confessed to a vicar that he had committed the Chorlton murder. William was freed on the condition he went back to Ireland which he did after one last visit to Chorlton, staying at the Royal Oak. Charlie was 'turned off' at 9 o'clock on 25 February 1879, still telling us he was not a bad man, just unlucky. Time has softened his image, and some see him as a folk hero, but he was really a twisted man who had a strange command over women (usually young) and animals: it was said that dogs never barked when Charlie burgled a house.

On the right is Wilbraham Egerton, Lord Egerton of Tatton. Created an Earl and Viscount Salford in 1897 in Queen Victoria's Diamond Jubilee celebrations, he died without children in 1909 and the titles died with him. This man played a large part in the forming of Chorlton, and it was he who insisted in keeping the chief rents on the land when it was sold off for building. On his left is Sir William Cunliffe Brooks, who lived at Barlow Hall for many years. He was a strong supporter of the 'old' parish church, and a giver of much time and money to good works in Chorlton. Born in 1819 in Blackburn, he took up the reins of his father's banking business in 1842. Until 1844 the bank issued its own notes, and for many years Sir William could be seen, at eight o'clock each morning, walking or riding his horse to work in the King Street Bank. He had a house in Scotland and a villa on the shores of the Mediterranean as well as his home at Barlow Hall, and was for many years MP for part of Cheshire. He married twice and had two daughters.

On the right is a portrait of Sam Mendel, drawn by Tidmarsh. Sam was a good businessman, and he made a lot of money, as Manley House and Park show. He was very unfortunate not to find backers or friends in Manchester when he wanted to turn the house and gardens into a pleasure park, and it was his turning to London and a Mr Fuller, that brought everything crashing down, and the end of Manley Park. It was Sam who in 1865 opposed (along with Cunliffe-Brooks) the transfer of the parish church to the new St Clement's, and it was their power and money that held off the new Chorltonians, who wanted everything of importance on or around Wilbraham Road.

On the left is Dr Alexander Maclaren, who opened the Baptist church on the corner of Wilbraham Road and Sibson Road on 29 May 1907. Born in Glasgow in 1826, he came to Manchester in 1858, and apart from preaching tours in Australia and New Zealand he spent the rest of his life here. The church cost £4,700 to build and after he died it was re-named as a memorial to Alexander Maclaren. This slight man of sober bearing, yet full of restless energy, sprang to life when he stood up to speak. The church was pulled down in the early 1970s because it needed a lot of money spent on it, and the congregation joined with the Macfadyen church to become Chorlton Central Church in 1975.

In 1919 Sir John W. Alcock KBE, DSC, had the world at his feet, literally as well as actually, for he was 'king of the air'. The King had just given him a knighthood, he was the first man to pilot an aeroplane across the Atlantic, he had survived the horrors of the First World War, and the future looked bright. He rests here after an accident on 18 December 1919, when he was aged just twenty-seven, while delivering a plane to an exhibition in France. His wonderful achievements are recorded in the stone memorials put up by his mother and the aviation industry. Born on Chorlton's doorstep in 1892 (see p. 85), he rests on Chorlton's doorstep.

Daniel Adamson, born in 1820 in Shildon, County Durham, was a good engineer; he was one of life's grafters. Yet we forget that, and record him as the man who started the movement that gave us the Manchester Ship Canal. He wanted ordinary people to have a share in the profits that he knew would come from the project. Daniel died on 13 January 1890, before his project had been completed. The leadership was taken over (with money from bankers) by Wilbraham Tatton, mentioned earlier. Daniel lies here in peace, remembered, at least by me, as a man who fought for the ordinary people.
Inset: Daniel Adamson.

The grave of John Rylands, one of the giants of the nineteenth century. Cotton merchant, warehouseman, benefactor, this man was the very essence of goodness. The only puzzle in his life story is that his first and second wives are buried at Ardwick, yet he rests here with his third wife, Enriqueta Augustina. Maybe she knew that the Ardwick burial ground was to be turned into a playing field. It is a fitting monument to the man who did so much good, and who did it quietly with no fuss or ceremony. He paid for the Bible to be translated into many languages, he paid for orphanages to be built for the street urchins of Rome, was made a Papal Knight by the Pope, and given the 'Crown of Italy' decoration. He was born in St Helens on 7 February 1801 and died on 8 December 1888. *Inset*: John Rylands.

They say that Salford adopted L.S. Lowry, but when it comes down to it Laurence Stephen Lowry was born in Old Trafford (less than a mile from Chorlton's border) and lies buried here, right on Chorlton's doorstep. 'As in life so in death', and our hero has to be content with being remembered on the side of the cross put up over his grandparents' grave. He was born on 1 November 1887, and he lived to the age of eighty-eight, dying on 23 February 1976 at Woods Hospital, Glossop. *Inset*: Self portrait, L S. Lowry.

Southern Cemetery also provides space to remember the hundreds of babies who arrive too soon or who are stillborn. They are buried here, and recently a small memorial has been put in place in this quiet and sheltered spot, to commemorate those tiny visitors who did not really start their journey through life.

Romeo, Romeo, wherefore art thou Romeo Foster? Answer – here, with a very strange figure that represents death sitting on top of this very strange tombstone. Among the other 'famous' names lying near here are Wilfred Pickles ('Have a Go, Joe', and 'Put the money on the table, Mabel'), Ernie Marples (Sir Ernest Marples, Stretford-born Minister for Transport who gave us parking meters, road markings and the Highway Code; I think they should put double yellow lines around his grave), Sir Matt Busby (who survived the Munich air crash), Billy Meredith (the footballer who played for both City and United), Jerome Caminada (the original Sherlock Holmes), and Francis Collier (the great Methodist preacher).

An aerial photograph of Manchester Crematorium, 1931. Sixty years ago there was a lot of open and empty space around the Crematorium. The original building (the Old Chapel) opened for business on 22 August 1892, over a month before it was officially declared open. The land was bought from Lord Egerton for £750, and the chapel and cremator cost a further £6,000.

The Old Chapel just after opening. Selling the idea of cremation to the English was not an easy task. Among the early names associated with the Manchester Cremation Society, who pushed the idea forward, and the Manchester Cremation Company, who built the establishment, are some very prominent and interesting people – W.E. Axon, the great historian and librarian, and Richard Christie, founder of the hospital which bears his name; Richard Peacock, founder of Beyer-Peacock, the railway engineers, and the Duke of Westminster, who was the first President of the company.

The war memorial in Southern Cemetery, dedicated to all those who gave their lives so that we may live in a better world.

Finally, have you seen a £2 coin? It's a wonderful thing, bright, colourful and heavy, just like a real Coin of the Realm. Around the edge of those first £2 coins are the words 'Standing on the shoulders of giants'. Historians, local and national, good and otherwise, cannot do much when they stand alone. The only way you can see clearly into the past is by standing on the shoulders of the giants, the greats, of past history. Chorlton has had two great historians in its past – Thomas L. Ellwood from the 1880s and John M. Lloyd from the 1960s and '70s. I would like to acknowledge that I stood on their shoulders quite a bit while compiling this book

BRITAIN IN OLD PHOTOGRAPHS

SUTTON'S PHOTOGRAPHIC HISTORY OF TRANSPORT

To order any of these titles please telephone our distributor, Littlehampton Book Services on 01903 828800
For a catalogue of these and our other titles please ring Emma Leitch on 01453 731114